WORKING
ECONOMICS

HOW TO CREATE, USE, AND PRESERVE WEALTH

JEREMY PS

Contact Info:

Twitter: @AuthorJeremyPS

Instagram: @AuthorJeremyPS

Website: www.WorkingEconomics.com

The legal stuff:

ISBN: 978-1-7362492-0-8 paperback
ISBN: 978-1-7362492-1-5 eBook

CONTENTS

To improving our economies

WORKING ECONOMICS: INTRODUCTION

The purpose of this book is to explain and unscramble the subject of Economics.

This book has opinions, but also contains what I have found to be factual and useful information.

Economics has sort of become this clouded subject which requires a Harvard degree and years of schooling to understand. This is ridiculous since we live in an economic world and economics is part of our day to day life.

The word *economics* has had different meanings over time. In the early 1900's economics meant something different than Political Economics. Political Economics is the studying of an area's or nation's production, distribution, and consumption of goods and services. People would just say economics as a shortening of Political Economics, and eventually the other definitions sort of fell away from use. Most of the time someone says economics now-a-days they are really meaning Political Economics. The focus of this book is not Political Economics, but it does have applications in that arena.

Below is the definition we will be working with throughout this book:

ECONOMICS: The branch of knowledge concerned with creating, using, and preserving wealth. As a subject it would include the data necessary for an individual or business to be able to create the money necessary to be alive or stay open, as well as the formulas to achieve and maintain wealth. As a field of study it would include the research of markets or regions as to what causes people to purchase desired goods and services, how they pay for them, and the different paths money travels on or where it ends up. Economics is separate from politics. Economics can have an impact on politics, just as politics can have an impact on economics. People can learn this subject and use the basic data of economics to handle their own lives and not be reliant on the politics or political philosophies of others.

We will be taking that definition and using it as it applies to you, instead of just how it applies to a nation or market. We will look at how you can understand and use the knowledge of creating, using, and preserving wealth for yourself, your family and your business or groups. This book is called *Working Economics* because it will show you how to make the subject of economics work for you.

We will be spending less attention on "how the debt level increased by .15% while wages only increased by .005% for the City of San Diego..." and we will be looking more at how you, as an individual, can understand the basic Laws and fundamentals of money, finance and wealth and so create the kind of life or business you want.

In my dealings with others I have found that almost everyone I have ever met, which is many people, have not had a basic understanding of this subject. Without a basic understanding, they have had less than desirable effects in their life on the subject of finances.

I don't think I know a single person (except for a small handful of people from multi-generational rich families) that haven't had major financial issues at some point in their life.

Almost everyone I have known either has, or has had at some point, more debt than they can handle.

I've never met anyone who was truly and honestly satisfied with their current level of income, savings, and total assets.

Most people I have come across would put something having to do with money as their biggest concern or desire. Normally the next subject of importance following this was relationships, and then it was feeling like they didn't have enough time. I am not saying which subject is more important. I'm just stating what I have learned and what other people consider important after talking with many. Money is the big one.

Getting, using, and keeping money is not hard if money itself and the subject of economics, as it applies to you, is understood.

I try not to find blame with people who are having financial difficulties. Almost every time people are in these situations, they also don't understand the subject of making money or how to manage it in the slightest.

This is why when people get bailed out of an economic jam, they normally end up messed up again at some point later on - sometimes they don't, but oftentimes people find themselves in the same or similar messed up financial situations more than once.

Note, I said bailed out - as in assisted by something outside their normal day to day living. Often when people get themselves out of their own economic mess, they learned something or figured something out or had an "Aha!" moment. This not only led to their recovery but made it possible for them to avoid getting into another mess down the road.

An example is the people who get a large inheritance or win the lottery. They didn't learn anything regarding economics and so most times end up wasting more than desired, if not all of their riches. And on the reverse, there are those who have earned what most would consider a fortune and they do not lose it nearly as fast, if they lose any of it at all.

If only 5% of Americans were unable to afford a $1,000 emergency, I guess we could blame the 5% for financial irresponsibility. But the amount of people with not even $1,000 saved up is much more than 5%.

It is 70%. That is the percentage of Americans that have less than $1,000 in savings.

Not long ago, the average household income in the U.S. was $61,937. I am writing this during the COVID-19 Pandemic and so the numbers being reported on household income now is considerably less.

The average Consumer Debt is $137,729.

Consumer debt is where the debt is owed by an individual instead of a business and is normally used for things such as student loans, housing, cars, credit cards, personal loans, payday loans, store credit, etc.

I believe the currently used system of economics in the U.S., and the world, is flawed.

With so many people afflicted with financial difficulties, I couldn't help but wonder if it's the system that is at fault. It cannot be a freak and unfortunate coincidence that 70% of Americans have less than $1,000 saved.

It can't be coincidence that almost everyone you meet has more debt than savings, more debt than their income, and a debt large enough that it would take them years to pay off, if they ever pay it off.

Now, there is a problem with the above averages: they don't necessarily account for the individual. It doesn't account for you. So, let's account for you:

Do you have more debt than you would like?

Do you feel your level of income is less than desirable?

Do you have less in savings than you feel you should?

Do you have less assets than you would like?

Are you concerned about the economy?

If any of those are a *yes*, then you are missing a workable understanding of the subject of economics - the science of making, spending, and keeping your money. Read the rest of this book to learn what that is and how to use it.

If all of those are *no*, then I ask you to read and learn more of this subject so you may help others. You will get a new and different way of looking at finances.

This is not about a popular, or currently used economic philosophy, but something different entirely.

I am not some millionaire start-up founder who unlocked the secrets to money and then abandoned the company to sell the secrets instead. I also didn't interview 100 billionaires and am now offering their secrets never before shared. I am just someone who was tired of his own financial difficulties and set out to resolve them. I then talked with many, many people and learned why so many others also had financial difficulties. I found that the reason for these difficulties is because of a missing understanding about the things we will cover in this book.

I've seen people having problems and stress with money while continuing to do the things that cause them their trouble. I have used the principles in this book for a while now, with tremendous benefit in my personal financial life. I have now found myself with a little bit of time available and so decided to sit down and write this book for you and others.

You might not agree with everything here, and you don't have to, but I think you will get something useful out of reading this if you give me some of your time. Thank you for reading.

CHAPTER 1: IMPORTANT - MEANINGS AND CONCEPTS CLARIFIED

First and foremost an individual would need to have an understanding of the basic words used in this subject, as well as the core concepts. Without these defined or clarified it can make the rest seem hard to understand.

Many people I've talked with that had trouble with money had basic concepts not understood and getting them clarified made the whole subject much clearer for them.

This chapter is important. But if reading a long list of words and their meanings sounds boring to you then skip ahead. Just make sure to refer back as needed.

The definitions and concepts here might not be the most popular, or the ones from school textbooks, however they are workable and so I would say are valuable and useful meanings for these words.

Some might seem unimportant, or too simple for you. Or maybe you know these all already. Some of these terms are not used in this book, but they are defined here anyway as they have been hard to understand or have caused difficulties for some people.

Here they are:

ACCOUNT: A record of money deposited into a bank for saving or future withdrawals. It can also be a record with a business for future purchases paid in advance.

ALLOCATE: Distribute or mark money for a particular purpose. Money can be allocated and not yet physically removed from an account, but it can be considered as good as gone as it is already named for a specific expense.

ASSET: Something owned by a person or company that has value and can be used, sold, or exchanged with others. It can also be used towards debts or other commitments. In certain cases, assets increase in value over time. In other cases, owning the asset produces income for the owner.

BALANCE: This is the amount of usable money held in an account. For a credit card or debt this would be the amount of the debt that is owed. On a credit card it wouldn't be available credit, but the amount of money in debt that is owed.

BANK: A company that collects money deposited by customers for safe keeping and then uses the money collected to make investments - normally for the gain of the bank. Banks also use the money deposited by customers to make loans to other customers. Banks make small amounts of money from services and fees, but the main source of the money they have to use or lend is from money kept in the vault by customers.

BANKRUPTCY: When someone is declared bankrupt through a legal procedure, it means they are unable to pay their debts. When someone declares bankruptcy, they are to a degree forgiven of some or all their debts. In some cases, assets are taken and used to settle or pay off what debts are possible. Sometimes payment plans are set up for a period of time to pay back some of the money that was owed. When a debt is forgiven, that specific debt or loan is ended without being paid off fully.

BILL: Money owed for services delivered or goods purchased. Often, people have repeating bills such as their phone bill. Bills should not be considered as debt unless they are past due.

BOND: A legal document that acts as an agreement for a loan. It is a way for people to loan money to businesses or governments. On the bond includes the payments, payment schedule and when it is to be paid off completely. It is like the opposite of a person getting a loan from a bank. The government or business is getting a loan from a person or an investment group. Bonds themselves also carry a value and can be traded with other investors.

CAPITAL: Money or assets owned by a person or business that can be used for a particular purpose or for investments.

CASH: Actual money that can be immediately exchanged for something else.

COLLATERAL: Something given up as a security in case a loan fails to be repaid. There is an agreement that should the loan fail to be repaid, the lender gets to keep what was agreed upon as collateral.

CREDIT: The ability for a person or business to buy things before paying for them based on being trusted to pay for them in the future. Credit is like a reputation someone or a company holds with the business that offers them goods or services. Credit is often measured as an amount of money the business is willing to let someone purchase on credit.

CREDIT CARD: A card issued by a bank that allows the holder of the card to make purchases on credit with the bank. It can be used to make purchases much like money can.

CREDIT LINE (or line of credit): The amount of credit given to someone from a particular bank or business.

CREDIT SCORE: A number assigned to a person that indicates their ability to pay back a loan. Credit score is used frequently to determine the amount of a loan and the monthly payments. It is used when someone wants to buy or rent a house or get a car. It's used sometimes when someone enrolls in service from a utility company. Credit scores are kept and assigned by private organizations, not the government. Credit scores are influenced by things such as how long someone has been using credit, their total available credit lines, their number of on time monthly payments, and more.

DEBT: Something, almost always money, that is owed and needs to be repaid.

DEFLATION: Opposite of inflation. Prices go down and money is able to buy more than before.

DEMAND: The desire or need to buy goods or services by a person, business, market, or region.

DIVIDEND: Money that is paid out on a schedule, normally every 3 months, to people who hold a special type of stock in a company. Not all stocks pay dividends.

ENTREPRENEUR: Someone who starts and creates a business or business activity. Normally there is risk involved in starting a business, at least when it is compared to the stability of working for someone else.

ECONOMICS: The branch of knowledge concerned with creating, using, and preserving wealth. As a subject it would include the data necessary for an individual or business to be able to create the money necessary to be alive or stay open, as well as the formulas to achieve and maintain wealth. As a field of study it would include the research of markets or regions as to what causes people to purchase desired goods and services, how they pay for them, and the different paths money travels on or where it ends up. Economics is separate from politics. Economics can have an impact on politics, just as politics can have an impact on economics. People can learn this subject and use the basic data of economics to handle their own lives and not be reliant on the politics or political philosophies of others.

ECONOMY: The financial state of an area. The area can be a particular market, or city, or country, or even the whole planet if someone wanted to look at a bigger picture. When people talk about the economy, they are normally referring to the overall financial state of a physical area (such as the United States or San Diego). In this book we will also look at the word economy as it relates to particular markets, or fields of interest. With the internet, vastly distanced collections of people are able to connect independent of their physical locations, and so this addition to the definition has value.

EQUITY: The percentage of something that is owned and that can be sold or turned into cash. Equity in a business is the percentage of the business that someone owns. Equity in a house is the amount of the house that the person owns, based on the difference between the current value of the house and what is still owed on the home loan (for example if the home's current value is $100,000 and someone paid off half of it, they would have $50,000 equity in the house).

FINANCE: The management of money. It can also mean how something gets paid for.

FUND: An amount of money put together for a specific purpose or to purchase something.

GOODS: Items that satisfy people's desires, provide usefulness, or meet a demand. These are things that can be traded and transferred to other people, and can normally be transferred multiple times, as opposed to *services* which are typically not transferable.

INCOME: Money received, especially when on a regular basis or schedule.

INFLATION: Increase of the prices within an area or market. The money used in that area buys less than it could before. Example: The price of a gallon of milk going from $1 to $2. It now requires more money to buy the same thing.

INTEREST: The money that is paid as the cost for getting a loan. Interest is paid at set times according to a schedule. Normally interest is paid monthly, and it is normally a percentage of the total loan amount. The amount of interest due each month normally lowers as the remaining amount of debt gets paid off. Interest will be paid until the debt is paid off. Interest that is due gets added to the total amount owed and in cases where a monthly interest payment doesn't get paid, the amount of debt grows, even though no new money was borrowed. Example: A $100 loan comes with 5% interest to be paid monthly. This would equal $5 a month at the beginning. Let's say the first month's interest isn't paid. Now the debt has grown, and the borrower now owes $105. In this example the required monthly payment has slightly increased as well.

INVEST: Putting money into something with the hopes of getting a profit as a result. Investments are the things that you put the money into to try to get a profit.

LATE FEE: Normally a loan has some sort of penalty for late monthly payments included as part of the loan agreement. If the monthly payment and interest isn't made by a certain date, then this fee is now owed as well - increasing future interest payments if not immediately paid. For some borrowers, paying this fee immediately isn't possible due to whatever caused the person to miss the last monthly payment.

LIABILITY: It is something a person or company owes, often an amount of money. Often, liabilities are resolved over time and cost money along the way. Sometimes the amount owed increases over time.

LIFESTYLE: The way someone lives their life and the things they spend money on to support their way of living. In the book I often say "fund lifestyle" and this means spending money on the things that allows someone to live the way they do, and often in a way that is more than just their needs.

LIQUID: Wealth owned in cash or in assets that can be quickly turned into cash. People whose wealth is not liquid might have millions of dollars in assets but be unable to use or access their money quickly.

LOAN: Something that is borrowed and expected to be completely returned by a certain time - most often this is an amount of money.

MARGIN (OR PROFIT MARGIN): The percentage of every dollar from a sale that turns into profit. If $100 is sold and the profit is $20, then there is a 20% profit margin. Profit Margin is one of the figures some businesses use to measure their success.

MARKET: A particular area of interest where similar goods and services can be classified together and where there is exchange of money for these types of goods and services.

Examples would be the laptop computer market, real estate market of San Francisco, or the real estate market of Milwaukee, WI, or the fine art market of Northern Seattle. There can also be sub-markets within markets. For example, the business laptop market, within the laptop market, or the luxury homes market within the San Francisco real estate market.

MARKETING: Promoting and selling products or services, doing market research, getting materials to potential buyers to inform them of a product or company and advertising. It is getting customers to want the services or goods and wanting to buy them.

MONEY: Something that represents value and can be given in return for something else considered of value. Money is a representation of all the things the people in a society consider valuable. They have trust that its value will stay true and be upheld by others. If they don't trust it, it loses value. Different cultures and civilizations have used different currencies or forms of money over time, but it all boils down to something to represent other things of value, such as hours worked is worth X amount of money, or a new TV is worth X amount, or a new house is valued at X.

MUTUAL FUND: A professionally managed collection of money from various different people that is pooled together and used to trade stocks. This money and the trades are managed by a company.

NET WORTH: The total value of someone's cash and assets combined, minus liabilities.

PERSONAL FINANCE: The management of someone's own money. Normally when someone says this term, they are also including investing and future planning.

PRINCIPAL: The original amount of money that is loaned at the time it is loaned.

PRIVATE (Company): A company where the stock is only available to the owners and people they choose to sell stocks to directly.

PROFIT: When the money gotten back from an activity or exchange is more than the cost to deliver or purchase originally, then there is a profit. The profit would be the amount of money remaining after the costs were taken out. For example, if it costs someone $40 to paint a fence, and the person gets paid $100 - there is a $60 profit ($100 pay minus $40 cost equals $60 remaining). Another example is if someone did work for someone else with no cost to deliver and got paid $100, then it would be $100 profit. As a note: just because profit does not factor in time as part of the cost, doesn't mean you shouldn't think about time involved when making financial decisions.

PUBLIC (Company): A company which offers stocks which can be bought by people with no connection to the owners of the company. These stocks are traded in the stock market and anyone can buy them.

QUALITY OF LIFE: Someone's level of health, comfort, happiness, and general wellness. Things that add to quality of life increase these things.

REAL ESTATE: Property consisting of land or buildings.

RESERVES: Money kept available and removed from the rest of available funds for other purchases and expenses. Reserves are often allocated for a particular future purpose or in preparation for one, such as an emergency. Reserves do not get used or tapped into to pay bills or purchases - unless that was the point of the reserve. A person or business can have multiple reserves, and it's smart to have multiple, each for different purposes.

RETURNS, RETURN ON INVESTMENT (ROI): This is profit received back from an investment. This is used by most to measure the level of success of an investment.

RICH: Having a lot of money. Being wealthy.

SAVINGS: Cash someone has collected, and it has not yet been spent or allocated.

SERVICES: An exchange in which no goods are transferred from the seller to the buyer. Something is purchased and delivered that cannot be traded again to someone else. Services would be things such as labor, help, consulting, counseling, education, events, construction, entertainment, legal services, transportation, communication, etc.

STOCKS: A representation of a piece of a company. A company can be broken down into smaller pieces called SHARES. The amount of shares a company can be split into is not dependent on the size of the company. A 2-person company could have 1 million shares, and a million-person company could have 2 shares. All the shares combined would equal 100% of the company. When someone is trading in stocks they are trading in pieces or percentages of the company. In theory if someone was to buy 5% of all the shares in a company, they now own 5% of that company. However, in reality this almost never makes the person 5% owner of the company - they just now own 5% of the shares. There are different types of stocks and it is set up in certain ways so that the average person gets their particular type of stock that is not the same as the people who actually own and run the company. The vast majority of stocks and stock trading is this kind, where it is exchanged between average people for money and has little actual value besides that.

Sometimes owning stock can get someone a percentage of the earnings of the company, but usually not. Stocks are usually exchanged for money and to this degree function similarly to money. People often buy stocks hoping that the perceived value increases and at a later time can be sold for more money than they bought the stock for originally.

SUPPLY: Goods or services available to be purchased or traded. Supply can also refer to the actual amount of goods or services available.

VENTURE: A business that involves a high level of risk. The perceived risk is normally in the beginning or formative stages.

VENTURE CAPITALIST: An investor that provides capital for small businesses or ventures for a percentage of ownership. These are seen as risky investments, but these types of investments can have the chance for massive returns.

WEALTH: A very large amount of valuable possessions or money. If someone is wealthy, then they have a lot of valuables or money.

CHAPTER 2: MODERN ECONOMICS AND A BRIEF HISTORY LESSON

We're going to take a look at what is currently being taught, and how economics currently exists in our society.

We are going back in time for a little history lesson. No doubt a history professor could school me on the "complete inaccuracy" of the following.

We'll begin this brief history lesson in the mid 1700's. In that time there lived a man named Adam Smith, of Scotland. Adam Smith is often referred to as the father of modern economics. He published a book entitled "The Wealth of Nations" in 1776. In a nutshell, he taught that all people operate out of self-interest and the basis of their work is for what it can do for them. His book is often referred to as the Bible of Capitalism.

Capitalism is an economic, and also political, system that involves using capital (as loans or investments) and making money from the interest of the loans or investments. The actual capitalist is not a business owner or producer, but more of a lender or investor. This is different from what is commonly taught or instructed, but this book is not about politics, and so we'll skip going further into what capitalism is.

In the mid to late 1800's Karl Marx finished his three main publications which he collectively entitled "Das Kapital" and with it Communism was born. Socialism in practice had existed before these works, but he expanded on it as an economic and political philosophy.

Communism is where the people in charge, or government, control all trade and money. They take the things that people produce and then distribute or sell it and get to keep the money created as a result. There are often limited rights of the people and they are severely controlled by the governing body.

Socialism is, according to Karl Marx, the social state between the overthrow of Capitalism and Communism taking over. In Socialism the government takes what is produced and gives everyone a piece, including the owner of what was taken.

Moving into the first half of the 1900's we have Lord John Maynard Keynes. He created what is called Keynesian Economics. He taught that you needed to create demand for goods and services. He instructed the government to increase its expenses and lower taxes on lower income earners in an effort to stimulate an increased demand. This was the idea that if people had more money, then they would want to spend it. This has been referred to as demand-side economics and has a focus on the lower and middle class. Basically, the idea is to do things from a governmental stance to try to get the people who purchase and consume goods to do so. This approach has led to large debts beyond people's ability to easily pay and increased inflation.

In the later half of the 1900's we switched focus to supply-side economics. This economic philosophy is in conflict with the demand-side of Keynesian economics. Basically, it's tax-cuts for big business and lessening of regulations with the idea of stimulating increased supply of goods from large businesses. The hope was that with more goods available people will then want to buy more of them. The belief was that with a larger supply of goods and services, there would be lower prices and more employment.

This system in application actually increased inflation, reducing the purchasing power of the dollar, and also increased the debt load of the government as well as the citizens.

At the end of the 1900's and start of the 2000's we had the massive rise of venture capitalism - it already existed before, but now there was a crazy amount of new companies forming out of thin air. These companies were being massively funded by investors in the hope that the value of the companies they invested in would skyrocket and they would hit a huge jackpot. This period in time is called the dot com bubble and it resulted in a market loss of $1,700,000,000,000 ($1.7 Trillion) from the crash in stock values.

In the end of 2007 we got The Recession, crash of the real estate market due to unqualified loans and overleveraged debts. It had a ripple effect across the banks, stock market, and available jobs.

Moving forward from The Recession and onward there is another massive explosion of venture capitalism in the realm of tech start-ups. Massive bets are made to the tunes of millions and more, not expecting the companies to succeed, but hoping one of the companies purchased will sky-rocket in perceived value of future potential investors.

There is an entire economic system based on the tech-start up. I've met and talked with hundreds of founders of start-ups in the San Francisco bay area - and not one of them was profitable. Yet almost all of them already had been given millions of dollars by investors and were now attending conventions to get more money.

In their presentations there was no mention of a plan to make a profit. A lot of them didn't even have a plan to make money from their business. But all of them had a plan to increase the perceived value of the company in the eyes of future potential investors and a plan for the founders and current investors to sell and get the hell out of the company with positive returns.

There are many companies valued at millions of dollars, and some at billions, that don't come close to making a profit. There are many that don't even make money!

The massive car-for-hire and food delivery service company Uber had a loss of $8.5 Billion in 2019. They have never made a profit since they were started in 2009, and to me it looks like they will continue to operate at a loss for some time. They have $65.5 Billion worth of stock being traded and owned. As you can see the real value of Uber is not the money it makes or can make - but the perceived value to investors.

This story, of a company not being able to survive on its own, but being worth millions or billions is repeatedly told - again and again and again and again.

This is no secret. In fact...

This is the business model!

With the continued rise of social media and self-promotion, people have been seeing the amazing success stories of companies and individuals making millions of dollars seemingly out of nowhere.

The stories don't involve the person creating and delivering things of value and earning their money that way, but by being involved in an exciting start-up, or from investing.

It has created an expectation in the people of my generation to get in fast and get out faster, *rich.* Or to get their money for nothing. YouTube is covered with ads of "How I made $17 Million last year from my couch and I'm only 19 years old."

And for those that can't figure out making their millions from hotel rooms in exotic travel destinations, there are always credit cards and loans. As I said in the intro, almost everyone has more debt than they can comfortably pay off. Many people use these debts for purchases to show off their success while they are "building their start-up." These are things like expensive vacations, computers and tech toys, and really nice but expensive Instagram posts.

End result: Massive debt, low to no income.

This system is a house of cards.

CHAPTER 3: THE LAWS OF ECONOMICS

Economics is actually simple. It is made complex on purpose. So those who understand the fundamentals are rich and those who don't, aren't. It was made complex long ago and is maintained to remain complex. How? Through education in schools and college. I'll leave off on that for now, so we don't go down some conspiracy hole chasing the white rabbit.

A law is a statement of fact that things are a specific way or happen a certain way every time if certain conditions are met. An example is the law of gravity, where if something goes up in the air it will fall back down.

The below are the Laws of Economics.

Economic Law #1: Demand is the desire or need for goods or service by anyone or any business. Demand can be from the individual, or from a group of individuals or a market. A market demand is the collective desire or need of a similarly classified group of individuals. Individuals act on desires or needs and make decisions for a business - a business itself is incapable of making decisions or acting on a demand.

Economic Law #2: Supply is the available goods or services to meet a possible demand. A supply by itself does not have actual value until it is available and is being traded or sold.

Economic Law #3: The existence of a demand is not enough for a supply to be developed or sold.

Economic Law #4: An increase of demand does not cause an increase of supply. Just as an increase of supply does not now cause an increase in demand.

Economic Law #5: The strength of the demand is in ratio to the perceived increase in ability to live or quality of life for the purchaser (even if only imagined). The more necessary something is to someone's ability to live or their quality of life, the stronger the desire is to have it. Scarcity can have an impact on demand on the basis that the buyer considers they need the product to increase their quality of life, and that there is limited availability or threat of losing availability.

Economic Law #6: The perceived value of a good or service is based on two primary factors: 1) Availability based on the existing supply and 2) Economic Law #5. The first factor is what regulates price in a market.

Economic Law #7: Inflation (reduction in the value of money and less purchasing power) occurs when there is more demand than there is supply.

Economic Law #8: Deflation (increase of purchasing power of money) occurs when there is more supply than there is demand.

Economic Law #9: Inflation and deflation do not occur naturally. Changes in the value of money is caused by changes in the supply or demand within a market and nothing else. Inflation and deflation occur within specific markets and industries and not just political zones or regions.

Economic Law #10: Money is itself a tradeable good. It can be traded and used to get more money. A currency goes as far as the people who use it believe in it. Investing money into something doesn't guarantee that there will be a return. However, by using money wisely, returns can be increased or speeded up. Money that is not allocated will eventually disappear. People and businesses find a way to spend more than they make and so unallocated money will eventually get spent.

Economic Law #11: If people do not know the existence of a good or service offering, they will not buy it - even if they are starving for it. If others are not made aware of your goods or services, they will not buy from you.

Economic Law #12: Your success in business is based on your ability to find, create or strengthen a demand, having goods or services to meet the demand and getting them marketed, sold and delivered in volume and with high quality.

Economic Law #13: If the goods or services delivered are different than what was expected, the purchaser will look elsewhere if they still have a demand. If you falsely advertise, your customers will look to your competitor.

Economic Law #14: Without marketing, there will be no business. The more potential buyers within your market that know of you, of your supply, and think of you - the better off you will be.

Economic Law #15: Sales is the bridge between Marketing and the purchase. Without a sales staff or system, purchases of a product are being lost.

Economic Law #16: The more the prospect with a demand understands the product, the easier the sale. Just as the less the prospect understands the product, the harder the sale. Increasing understanding can help increase demand if the increased understanding shows them how the product can increase their quality of life.

Economic Law #17: Price only affects a demand in a market when there are alternative goods or services available. When a purchase is made, the buyer often considers how the price will affect their quality of life. Some consider a higher price a better purchase and some consider a lower price a better purchase - but only when there are alternatives.

Economic Law #18: Government and politics do not belong in business. Changes to laws (as in rules and regulations), or new ones introduced, by the government can have short-term negative or positive effects. But in the long run, government involvement in business will create negative effects.

Economic Law #19: Breaking the law (as in rules and regulations), or side-stepping it, can ruin your business and life. Being above boards in all dealings, and continually documenting the fact protects you and can make you bulletproof.

Economic Law #20: Government and politics will always try to change the economic systems in use or develop new ones.

Economic Law #21: A business without profit will fail unless it starts making a profit. Its ability to make a profit depends upon the cost to make, market, and deliver goods or services and is multiplied by the volume of the goods or services sold and delivered.

Economic Law #22: Something sold without the delivery of the goods or services as they were expected is what causes a desire for refund.

Economic Law #23: A person or business without a regular addition to a reserve account is likely to fall into debt. Debt is not guaranteed, but there is no safeguard against becoming indebted without a reserve account set up and being added to.

Economic Law #24: Financial security is based solely on having more income than expenses, plus regularly adding to reserves. Financial security and survivability are then increased by maintaining and increasing income, lessening expenses or money going out, and continually adding more to reserves.

Economic Law #25: A business's previous customers are its best source of future income. The highest amount of money to be made is from previous satisfied customers. Keeping records of previous customers and their purchases is worth its weight in gold.

Economic Law #26: If a business does not continue to get new customers added to its customer-base then it will eventually go out of business.

Economic Law #27: The Laws of Economics are applicable to personal finance, business, governments, nations, etc. Anywhere there is an exchange of money for goods or services these Laws apply. They have exact applications that give exact results. Economics is not complicated and can be understood and applied by all. The creation of and keeping of wealth is dependent upon the following of these Laws, whether they are known about or not. The more Laws that are understood and applied, the more certainty and stability a person or business will have. The more they are violated the less stability and certainty possible.

And there you have it. This is the core of the book. If someone were to apply these and find ways to energetically align their lives and businesses to these Laws, they will generate wealth and be able to maintain it with certainty and stability.

CHAPTER 4: FALSE ECONOMICS & FALSE ADVICE

Now that we have looked at the Laws of Economics, we will be getting into the wrong or unworkable principles that you and many others have been sold on or taught.

Why have you been sold wrong data? For the profit of others. Some of the most common wrong data has to do with investments and the stock market. Let's dive in.

When there are gains in the stock market - the money came from somewhere. The money didn't just materialize.

When someone wins big in the stock market - it is not a generation of wealth, but *a transfer of wealth*.

Stock market investors make their money at the expense of other investors. These other investors are made up of other bankers, business owners, laborers, mothers, fathers, cousins, children, and the rest of the people who put money into the stock market.

When a big firm cashes out $1.5 Billion dollars, that is a transfer of wealth, not a generation of wealth. This is a transfer of wealth to them, from the other investors listed in the above paragraph collectively.

This might just be the biggest misconception regarding investments and stocks. That money into the stock market somehow generates more money - this is false. Money invested in a company is not used by that company to make profits to send back to investors. Money put into stocks and the returns from the market are only a transfer of wealth.

An increase of value in a stock comes from Economic Law #6 (The value is based on availability of the existing supply and perceived potential increase in quality of life for the investor.) The increase of value in a stock does not come from the company itself doing better or making more profit - but from Law #6 only. With the increase of the perceived value of a stock, someone is now willing to pay more money for the stock than you did and so you get more money back.

Again, a transfer of money - not the generation of money.

Generation of money comes from Economic Laws #12 and #27 (**#12:** Your success in business is based on your ability to find, create or strengthen a demand, having a service or goods to meet the demand and getting it marketed, sold and delivered in volume and with high quality. **#27:** Anywhere there is an exchange of money for goods or services these Laws apply. They have exact applications that give exact results.)

It is impossible for someone to make a gain in a stock without someone else having a loss. Again, for the fifteenth time, it is a transfer of wealth not the generation of it.

Millions of people invest with the hopes that the money they put in will grow and result in more money. They do their research and make their picks. They send in their money and get their confirmation that the trade was successful. They watch hopefully. As time goes on, they see the value go up. They see the $10,000 they put in is now worth $10,500. This is a $500 profit! At this rate it will be worth $15,000 in several years!

Several years go by. The big banks and big investment firms see that the price of this particular stock, which they also invested in, hits their desired price goal and so they sell. They make a fat profit too. With the money coming out and more shares of this company becoming available from their sale (the supply increasing) the price of the stock goes down.

Suddenly the small-time investor who was hoping to hit his $15,000 sees that his stock is now worth only $6,000. He has lost all his earnings plus an additional $4,000 from his initial investment.

In fear of losing more money he SELL SELL SELLS his stock and gets out before it's too late. As time continues, he sees the value go down even further, and he finds a little comfort in the fact that he sold and only lost $4,000 instead of losing $8,000 if he had waited until later. Oh, what luck. At least he still has the $6,000 to re-invest when he feels the time is right.

With the new low price, the big investment firm from before comes back and buys another large amount of stock in this same company. This then begins to drive the stock price back up.

This little story plays out like a recording, endlessly on repeat.

It happened big in the 2007-2009 recession. A lot of people lost their savings and money, but the money went somewhere - some people made out like bandits and made out BIG. Again, it is a transfer of wealth.

It happened again very recently on the whole Bitcoin craze if you remember that. Tons of people poured their money in, trying not to miss out on this new and exciting opportunity. Several made out like bandits at the expense of the new investors coming in - transfer of wealth.

Now why do I keep banging this drum?

Because we have all been taught and reminded and reminded again, that the key to our financial future is to put our money into investments. What that really means is the stock market or similar, traditional investments. We are sold on this idea from a youngish age and reminded constantly.

Lobbyists (professional influencers of political officials) affect governmental regulations to make it make more sense for you to take some of your income and put it into investments or special accounts at the bank - you get tax write-offs in some such cases.

You are continually marketed to about it through TV and radio.

Financial gurus continue to sell you on this.

It all traces back to the big-time banker.

The big-time banker makes his wealth off of the people.

People put their money into the bank for safekeeping. The bank then uses their money to make investments - for the profit of the bank. These investments generate returns for them, which is really more money being transferred from other ordinary people or other banks. Their investments result in an additional transfer of wealth from the people back to the bank.

The banks get wealthier. And the people get a little less wealthy.

The conventional wisdom of investing and the need to invest is really the filtered down sales pitches from the Big Banks. The Big Banks appear rock solid and totally stable as they are applying Economic Law #24 (Financial security and survivability is increased by maintaining and increasing income, lessening expenses or money going out, and continually adding more to reserves.)

Now, the truth of the matter is if it works for them it *could* work for you. But it is not guaranteed, and chances are slim. There are undoubtedly people who have gotten rich from stocks, but those stories are far, far, far fewer than those who lost big.

The banks are selling you on a workable system - workable for them. And really, only consistently workable *for them*. Banks are really the only ones (other than a small selection of people) who have consistently made positive returns from stocks. And even the banks eventually lost!

Big Banks lost hard in 2008, but they got bailed out by the government. The big difference is that you don't have the same insurance policy! How many times has the government bailed out the average citizen who made poor investment choices or suffered from a severe market crash? You won't get bailed out when you lose it all like the banks did.

It is for all of these reasons that I am against using the stock market as a tool to build wealth. The rich don't even use stocks to build wealth. They make their wealth by other means and then use stocks to build upon the wealth they already have.

If you absolutely have to use stocks because if you don't your mom and dad will be mad and disown you, then wait for a crash, put some money in and forget about it for several years or forever. But that is easier said than done as repeatedly seen over and over again throughout the last hundred years.

Next, we have the magic of compound interest. This is recited and taught and sold over and over again. People quote Albert Einstein as having said *"Compound interest is the eighth wonder of the world."* Compound Interest is the math that when you take earnings from interest and re-invest them into the same investment it grows and earns even more interest.

Compound interest is a true and factual thing. The math is real at least. If you have $10,000 at 7% interest per year, re-invested every pay-out and the interest doesn't change then you will double your $10,000 and have $19,990 at the end of 9 years.

Here is the issue with this principle in the stock market: It is too unpredictable. People have charts and metrics and formulas for predicting the market. All these analysts, except a few, said the market was going to continue its climb through 2008 and even said it would continue through 2009. They were wrong, very wrong. They were so wrong, yet people still listen to them today!

Einstein did also say, to continue his quote on compound interest, *"He who understands it, earns it ... he who doesn't ... pays it."* Or in other words, by not understanding it you end up being the one paying it to others.

All too often people blindly follow whichever salesman is pitching them on this concept and invest into (insert next big stock named to be a winner here). They don't understand it and so they pay it - AGAIN, transfer of wealth.

Compound interest is not a sure thing in the stock market. People who say otherwise have something to gain for selling this idea, or they are repeating what they have already heard.

Compound interest does in fact work and it works best for bankers and big-time investors. A bank loans you money to buy a house or car and then takes the money that you pay them as interest and re-invests it into more loans. Boom! Compound interest at work.

But for the little guy, he takes from his earnings and what he can scrape together and throws it into the stock market. He takes any investment returns and re-invests. Overtime he sees some promise. The initial investment is growing, and he is adding to it. After several years there is a correction of the market and the value of his stocks take a small, but steep dive. He panics - and sells. He ends up with a gain overall and is pleased but swallows some disappointment. He now has this money - more than he had before, a success! He knows he is supposed to re-invest and so picks some more stocks and invests. Over the next several years there are some dips and also some rises, but overall, by the end of 9-10 years he is slightly ahead. He gets frustrated and remembers the old risk-vs-reward rule and makes some bigger bets. He loses. He gets frustrated and forgets about it.

We've all heard of those 13-year-olds throwing their bar mitzvah money at penny stocks and making millions - but come on. Can that really be you? Are you even 13 years old?

There is of course the managed portfolio. Your mother gives her money to someone much smarter and better educated than you. This person has lots of clients and works for a big bank - he knows what he is doing. He sits in a very tall chair at his office, so it is easier for him to look down on everyone.

Your mom gives him her life's savings. He assures her he is going to take good care of her. He takes the money and puts it into conservative funds with little risks. As the years go on the money does stay above the rate of inflation, but barely. After fees and the advisor's cut for managing her money there are less gains than was hoped for.

"But my grandfather left me stocks in his will that are worth lots and lots of money after he invested in Coke back in the 1950's." Got it! We've all heard the story. There is a chance if you put your money into Coke today and forgot about it for the next 70 years it would be worth quite a lot and you can leave it for your grandkids. There's a chance it won't, or the company goes under. Either way I am not sorry to say: it is gambling.

"But what about the 19 year old day-trader on the YouTube ads selling his fool-proof day trading system and how he made millions and became an overnight success that no one has ever heard of?" Yeah, go ahead and buy his "fool-proof-system," but remember you have the same or better odds of winning instead of losing it all if you take up sports betting, horse racing, or coin tosses - literally. A coin toss is a 50-50 chance.

When it comes to stocks, people share with their friends the hot stock tips, investment advice, and tell stories of the times they made out big - they don't talk about the times they lost hard. It is the same for the trips to Las Vegas. Big wins have big stories. The same people don't volunteer to share the times they went bust and lost large amounts of money.

There are some exceptions, but in today's modern economy the ways of old just won't cut it - no matter how many times it's preached. A very long time ago stocks were often valued based on distribution of goods, income of the company, debts owed, and more. Today we have companies which have never made a dime valued at billions, and these are seen as good investments or at least good bets. They may be good bets, but again we are talking about perceived value vs actual value.

Have I made my point? Good.

If you actually know someone who earned an average income through their employment for their whole career and saved it all up, invested it into the stock market and now is successfully and comfortably retired, please contact me and let me know the story – I'm interested in hearing all of the details.

You might be thinking, *"But what am I supposed to do with the money I earn and don't spend on bills or fun?"* We will get to that later in this book, don't worry.

You might also be wondering what about other financial instruments set up by big time bankers to get your money, such as CDs (Certificate of Deposit - long term deposit with a small return), bonds (a fancy loan with a small interest rate where you get the payments from the borrower), REITs (Real Estate Investment Trust - a way to invest in real estate, except the bank owns the property instead of you), etc.

Here is a blanket statement: **The financial instruments employed by banks for you to invest your hard-earned money are set up to make them money, not you.**

Take a minute to let that sink in, think it over.

Many investment opportunities include a nice commission to the banker or financial advisor who convinced you what a great opportunity such and such mutual fund is, or some other investment. Sometimes these commissions are hidden so you don't even realize you are paying them.

Why would these big corporations, that need to prove to the Board of Directors that they made positive income this quarter, set things up that cost them money in order to make you money? That's right - they don't! Your financial well-being is fourth place to them in importance. For the banker priorities go: themselves, the board, the tax man (government), and then last and most often least, you - the client.

CHAPTER 5: HOW THEY GET YOU AND WHY

The first step in losing the economic battle is by being convinced you need more than you have in order to live.

This is a very simple statement. But this is the foundation that starts someone on the path to losing financially.

Since the beginning of time people have survived without having any money or only having a small amount.

The amount of people who actually starve to death within the U.S. is so low the numbers aren't even tracked. I'm not saying there isn't a hunger issue, or that some people and kids aren't poorly fed. I'm saying that very, very few people starve to death in America.

1,300 people in the U.S. die every year due to exposure (being outside during harsh weather without enough protection or shelter). This is out of the total US population of 328.2 Million people.

During the Great Depression (the worst economic point in US history starting in 1929 and lasting 10 years), deaths due to starvation or exposure did not increase. In fact, the life expectancy of people during this time increased by as much as 6 years.

Sorry to go all dark for a moment, but the truth of the matter is that in the U.S. the poorest of the poor can still be alive. Their lives might be miserable to them, but they are alive - and probably much better off than the majority of the population of this planet. I've known people with poverty level income who still had big screen TVs, cell phones, and more. These people weren't starving.

If you suddenly and literally lost everything in your life it would undoubtedly suck, but you wouldn't die as a result. You would still find a way to live.

Afterall, there was a time before the internet and supermarkets and cars and planes and farms and cell phones and TV and big business and banks. And people survived back then too!

All of this is not to suggest that people don't face tough circumstances or that all those who feel they got it rough just need "to suck it up and deal with it." I'm just pointing out that most everyone has, or can get, what they need to live.

Now, there are things that improve quality of life that could be argued as a necessity for living in this modern age. I would personally consider a cell phone to be a necessity - even though if mine disappeared I would still be alive. There will be more on the subject of expenses and necessities in a later chapter.

At a very young age we are introduced to this concept of money and the need to have it. We are shown the ads for the coolest toys or movies and how much better our quality of life would be if we had them. Our friends have the coolest and newest G.I. Joe or Barbie or Nintendo, etc.

At this very young age we are shown how we must have these things that we don't yet own. Maybe you don't remember this yourself, but I am sure you can think of a time you saw a young child that didn't get his or her way and the upset that followed.

As we grow up, we overhear and catch glimpses of the reality our parents live in. A reality of earning and paying bills and trying to save for the future.

It begins to sink in when we are faced with the *neeeeed* to go to college and we, along with our parents, don't have enough to cover the tuition.

And at this point is the first real big gotcha: *the student loan.*

We were convinced that this was necessary in order to live in the modern world. And with us so convinced of the need for it, and without having the available funds, we turn to the common and readily available solution that magically presents itself: *the student loan.*

It is of course a sour disappointment when the majority of us cannot find employment after finishing a long and sometimes difficult, but definitely expensive education.

Throughout our education (and often since back in high school) there is an exposure to the lifestyles seen being enjoyed by friends, or the lifestyles seen through social media that makes us feel like we are lacking or we are "have-nots."

We see the cute young couple taking their fourth vacation this year. We see the friend who can go out to the bar and pick up the tab every weekend. Or the young person with the super nice car.

We see these things and figure we must have these too in order to really be living. I mean look how happy they all are. Little do we know, they cannot afford these things either! Most of them are using debt in order to finance these purchases and lifestyles. But we don't know this. We just see the awesome pictures and figure they must have a wealthy family, or they just got lucky. Either way, we want to keep up and are convinced we need these things to be happy or live well, and this leads us to...

The second big gotcha: *credit card and other debt to finance lifestyle.*

Credit card companies will gladly allow you to take out more credit than you can reasonably make the payments on.

Moving forward a few years. After some chaos and finally landing a job that isn't too rotten you remember you are supposed to buy a house. Your parents had one, and so did their parents. This is what you are supposed to do. Didn't we all hear something about how unsmart it is to pay rent. It was something like you pay all this money and you don't even get to own what you have been paying for, or something like that...

So, we get up and go to the bank where we already took out a loan to finance our car and we apply for a home loan. It gets financed and we get locked in on paying them money for the next 30 years. *This is the third big gotcha.*

Each one of these major milestones end up shaping the lives of just about everyone you meet. I will explain this more in a moment, but first a short detour.

In 1955 an American musician by the name of Tennessee Earnie Ford hit the top of the music charts with his cover of *Sixteen Tons,* originally by country singer Merle Travis. Elvis Presley later did his own cover of this song, as did Johnny Cash and many others.

The song is about coal miners working themselves to death through very demanding and harsh physical labor, all while breathing in the toxic fumes from the coal mines. A line from the song goes over how the coal miners would spend a long and difficult day mining and loading coal, and by the end of the day they are somehow in even more debt. Saint Peter from Heaven can't call on them since they owe their soul to *the company store.*

The company store was a store owned by the coal mining company. They would sell food, clothing, cigarettes, alcohol, you name it - all on credit. The credit extended would nearly always exceed the miner's ability to pay. They would then be in debt to the company. See where this is going?

They would work a hard day, but by the end of it they would be in more debt from needing to buy things from the company store, which they bought on credit. The company in essence owned the miners. They couldn't leave or quit despite poor health conditions because they owed the company. Hence, the miner couldn't even afford to die and go to heaven as he was owned by the company store. This was not by accident.

The bank (including credit cards and lenders) is our *company store.*

It extends us credit so we can get the things we "have to have": education, lifestyle, transportation, housing, etc.

We are then indebted to them and though we aren't employees of the bank we do work for them indirectly. We work to earn so that we can repay our debts.

The majority of financial problems revolve around this point of trying to pay off or pay down debt.

Now, from a banker's perspective: Americans pay them on average over $8,000 per year, which is about 13% of their household income, in interest and fees.

Hopefully I don't lose you on the math here: The average size of a household in America is 3.14 people. There are 104,522,293 households. 104,522,293 X $8,000 per household equals $836,178,344,000.

Banks in the United States collectively make about $836 Billion dollars PER YEAR on interest and fees alone. This isn't even getting into investments, repossessions and re-sales, or any of the other ways they make money.

I am not trying to preach a "give-up your lifestyle philosophy" or "get rid of material goods." Quite the opposite actually. It isn't having things or wanting them that is the problem, but how we go about getting them. We go about getting these things the way we do because of how we've been educated and marketed to.

We went over how they got you. In terms of why? Look again at the $836 Billion per year they make as a result.

CHAPTER 6: 67 "WORDS OF WISDOM" AND WHY THEY ARE BULLSHIT (ALSO WHAT ABOUT THEM WORKS)

We have all heard the things that are common knowledge, or words of advice from billionaire investors from their golden thrones. They often get repeated and repeated, and spread around as smart advice, mostly without any real understanding of what is being repeated. Not all of them are bullshit, but we are going to go over some of the common ones.

PLEASE NOTE: This chapter was written with the intent to be skimmed. You can read the whole chapter if you want, but it is lengthy and could get boring. As a minimum, browse through and read the sections that grab your attention.

Before we start with the bullshit, a wise man once said, "Follow common advice and achieve common results." I strongly agree with this statement. Applied to personal finance, the common result is paying $8,000 per year in interest and fees, and having less than $1,000 in savings.

Live below your means: The concept is to live a lifestyle that costs less than you can afford so that you have more money left over. Overall, the concept is fair, but this often-repeated phrase is lacking in usefulness.

Why it's bullshit: It doesn't ensure or even focus on income and it does not consider adding to reserves. Please note, that reserves are different from just saving money.

What about it works: The statement does align, to a degree, with Economic Law #24 concerning financial security.

Invest in the stock market: This is the direction to take your earnings and put them into the stock market.

Why it's bullshit: See Chapters 4 and 5.

What about it works: If you bet big enough and often enough, there is a chance you could win. But don't forget that it is gambling. It's a hope for financial gain based on speculation of an increase in perceived value later on. Please don't mis-understand me: I'm not saying that no one ever hit it big in the stock market or that there aren't people living the good life because they bought Intel in the 80s. But, there are a lot of people who are still working in their "retirement years" because they lost their savings in some stock market crash or were persuaded to invest in a company that went bust.

Find and listen to finance podcasts and read blogs: There is a tremendous amount of information on this subject. Money and finance are a primary concern for most people and so there are a lot of people who have written and talked on the subject - me being one of them.

Why it's bullshit: There is so much out there. The existence of information doesn't mean it's valuable or useful or even worth the time to read and listen to. Further, there is a lot of misinformation in circulation. I have sorted through some of what's available and found that a tremendous amount of it simply repeats what someone else has already said (which isn't necessarily a bad thing). A lot of it pushes ideas that the first few chapters of this book attempted to explain were bad or false.

What about it works: There is some valuable information out there. Some of it is very valuable! But the problem is trying to find it and then trying to figure out if it actually is worthwhile. I would say if someone recommends a particular source of information on the subject of economics or personal finance, ask them where to go and why they recommend that source. Listen to their answer and then decide if it is worth your time. Continuing to educate yourself is definitely worthwhile, but not if you are spending time filling your head with garbage.

Save and Invest for retirement: This is the idea of starving yourself (financially) now so that you can "eat" decently when you are in old age.

What about it is bullshit: Withholding from yourself now sounds crappy doesn't it? Maybe someone is already doing it and has learned to live with it. "It's not so bad," someone might tell themself. Investments with this advice typically end up being stocks or other instruments by big bankers to get *your* money into *their* pockets. It's bullshit and sad for me to see people spend their lives funding these banks and then not ending up with an adequate amount to live the life they expected once they hit retirement age.

What about it works: People who have gotten company-matched investments into retirement savings that remained untaxed and untouched for 30-45 years and conservatively invested with a small gain leaves some people with enough to pay for a decent if not a good retirement. Now, we need to remember that retirement should be a regular life and should come with regular expenses, you're just not working.

Buy your house. Own where you live: The idea that rent is a waste since you are spending money and don't get to own anything. This idea is that you must pay the bank instead of a landlord because at the end of 30 years you will then get to own your property.

What about it is bullshit: You are tied to the property now for 30 years or until you sell it. The money you pooled together to go into this resource is now unavailable for other potential things such as income producers (more on income producers later in the book). Once paid off you still need to pay taxes, insurance, repairs and maintenance, and any fees when you need certain types of repairs or upgrades. For just about everyone, they will need a loan to buy a house and they end up buying in a market where the price is unfavorable.

What about it works: As the value of the home increases over time and eventually gets paid off after 30 years or so, and depending on any refinancing or additional loans against the property, people often get a decent chunk of change tied up in their house. This allows them to leave a decent inheritance to their children when they die. Additionally, when someone is certain they do not want to move again in the next 15-30 years, absolutely love the house they are looking at, see no circumstances needing them to change homes, and they time the market just right: it makes sense to own where you live. There is another additional benefit: When people have their net worth tied up in their home, they are less likely to spend this wealth wastefully than if this money was available to them as cash. Another nice perk is you can do whatever you want with the property, given that it fits within government regulations for your zone. There are of course other things involved in owning your home or real estate, and there is a little more on that later.

Buy the dip: This is the idea that when a stock goes down this provides an opportunity for you to get in on this particular stock. This comes with the idea that it is going to go back up. This is almost said as a joke.

Why it's bullshit: Again, see earlier parts on stocks. It is still gambling. "Buying the dip" has burned a lot of people. People have seen a big-name stock go down in price and instead of recognizing a possible crash in value, they seize their chance to get more shares for cheaper.

What about it works: I don't see any value with this datum. It is based on the idea that dips and rises are inevitable and if it goes down the next move is up. It reminds me of the concept some gambling people have with bets: if a coin is tossed and lands on tails four times in a row then on the next flip it has got to land on heads - it's silly. The odds are still the same with each following coin flip: 50-50. The stock market is all about odds and risks.

Quit while you're ahead: This is thinking that since you have done well and are in a better position financially that you should stop going in this direction before you have a loss.

Why it's bullshit: Because whatever is working for you can keep working for you. Keep cranking along and moving ahead being successful, Keep continuing to win, and get further ahead!

What about it works: If this is being thought of in terms of stocks, or some other financial instrument based on speculative growth - then yes, not a bad idea to quit while you're ahead. Just as if you were in a casino and you won a decent pool of cash, get out of there before the house takes it all back.

Cut your losses: This is when you recognize something you have been spending time or money on isn't going favorably. You might have been thinking that if you just keep at it, eventually it will turn around and you will get some sort of profit. Then someone tells you to give up before you lose even more and "cut your losses."

Why it's bullshit: Because an assessment of the actual scene would need to be done and honestly worked out to determine if it's time to let something go or not.

What about it works: When it is recognized that some activity or effort is draining profits and parasitic on income without any reasonable hope of it turning around in the future, then it should be eliminated without hesitation.

Fail fast: This is a business idea that when a business is not going too well to let it die rapidly, or even kill it, so that you can go off onto the next business.

Why it's bullshit: Someone should always do market research before getting into any business. They should have found a demand and then created a business with the goal of supplying that demand. Further, marketing does take time, and getting your product known about and people wanting it doesn't happen in a minute. I believe that this idea of failing fast has prevented a lot of people from getting to the point of success.

What about it works: When someone recognizes they are in a sinking ship where there is no way of getting any repairs, the walls are busted with water gushing in, and there is no way to plug the hole and get it going right again - then yes, get out fast, smoothly, legally, and honestly. You don't go down with the ship. Since this isn't actually a ship we are talking about, but a metaphor for a business: there is no honor or sense in a business owner going down with the business in shame, or losing his/her personal savings while still failing. We're not talking about a literal captain staying onboard his literal sinking ship.

All debt is bad. Never get into debt: The idea that someone should never touch debt or think of debt as an option and avoid it all costs.

Why it's bullshit: If someone was going to starve, they would use debt to get food. Using debt can make sense when there is an actual and definite return on the purchase, and the return was boosted by getting it now. For example if productivity and income could be increased by removing the time necessary to earn the funds needed, and the increased return was sufficient to justify not waiting to earn the amount needed first, borrowing could make sense. Where the increased value of getting it now was greater than the cost of taking on and then paying off the debt, then using debt can be a good option. Such a calculation should consider all the costs of the debt being taken on including fees, interest, collateral if used, etc. More on this in a later chapter.

What about it works: For people without discipline, or who are unwilling to use discipline on the subject of finance, then it can be a blanket datum that can give them a feeling of stability or keep them from being overwhelmed by debt. It also works regarding using debt to finance lifestyle. I can't think of any circumstances where using debt to finance lifestyle makes sense.

Pay off your credit cards as fast as possible as the priority: Here is the idea that if you have credit card debt you must be a sucker or were a sucker in the past. That you need to get rid of it now no matter what. That you should pool all possible resources into getting rid of the debt as fast as possible. While there is a lot of value in eliminating credit card debt, people have gone overboard on this piece of advice with self-sacrifice to speed up the process.

Why it's bullshit: For most people, getting rid of their credit card debt as fast as possible will require sacrificing other things. Expenses should be cut, but I'd argue: not at the cost of negatively impacting personal well-being. Don't starve or eat improperly to have an extra couple hundred bucks to throw at the credit card debt. Yes, cut expenses where possible, and yes get rid of the debt - but not by making yourself miserable to do so. You don't need to teach yourself a lesson for racking up the debt in the first place. 0% interest offers for a limited time are available, like a year, and these can hold your debt while you pay it off so that you are not getting hit so hard with interest.

What about it works: Credit card debt is very expensive. Most cards today charge between 18 and 24% interest per year. This is an insane amount of money to pay for the "privilege" to use these credit cards. A $5,000 debt on a credit card with 18% interest would have a minimum monthly payment of about $200. If just the minimums were paid it would take just over 11 years to pay it off and would cost a total of $7,873.51.

Trust the pros, the financial advisors and investment bankers: This is about putting your faith in the banker or financial advisor to manage your money.

Why it's bullshit: It is your money! You would be giving it over to someone who makes a living from using other people's money. It has been normal for so long that people don't see the silliness in this. There is almost nothing a financial advisor can do for you that you can't do on your own. The only advantage they have is more time in the game or understanding of what investments to choose - but you can learn these on your own with some time. Using a financial advisor to make investments for you just takes the responsibility away from you and replaces the need to learn with an ignorance of what is happening with your money.

What about it works: You have someone else to blame if you lose your money. Sometimes an advisor can connect you with people or opportunities that would be hard to find otherwise.

Automate your bills: Setting up auto-pay or automatic withdrawals to pay your bills at fixed times.

Why it's bullshit: You take your finger off the pulse of your finances. Doing this can leave you less aware of what is happening with your money. If your income is much greater than your expenses you probably won't feel it, but for people who already barely make ends meet this can make it even harder. They look at their bank account balance and see what money they have and make plans to use the money. Sometimes people forget that there are automatic withdrawals coming soon. At times, the automatic withdrawals occur and are forgotten about leaving the person with overdraft penalties and these end up costing the person more. Keeping the responsibility and taking the few minutes to pay bills while waiting for something else during your day, or using the bathroom is not difficult. It keeps you fully aware of all your money going out. If someone is afraid of missing payments, then reminders can be set to pay before the due date - your phone has such a reminder feature. The real benefit for the automatic payments is for the people who are owed. They get assurance that the bills will be paid and that your money will get to them. Don't underestimate the value in seeing where every penny goes. It's this level of awareness that places you fully in control of your finances and financial options. *You spend so much time making the money, why not spend just a little bit of time managing it.*

What about it works: Sometimes companies offer discounts or incentives if they are on autopay. Saving a few bucks by enrolling doesn't hurt. As an example, I am auto enrolled on my gas bill, so I don't have to pay them the extra fee they enforce if I wasn't.

Never use your credit card unless it's an emergency: This is having credit cards for the only purpose of being able to come up with money for an emergency.

Why it's bullshit: Some credit cards have good introductory offers. These used correctly, and paid off have earned people vacations, flights, cash back, meals, etc. Simply using a credit card doesn't harm you. Owning and using a credit card will not hurt your finances, as long as you practice discipline and don't fund lifestyle or make wasteful purchases. Further, people should have money stashed for an emergency before the emergency happens. We'll go over setting up reserves for such things in Chapter 8.

What about it works: For people who can't practice discipline or aren't willing to learn the science of Economics, or at least get an understanding of personal finance, then this is an alternative. But it is not a good alternative, it takes financial responsibility away. It would be like saying "because I can't exercise financial discipline, I'll just make it so I don't have to." While this can work for some, it's far better to be in control and fully responsible for all financial decisions.

Budget 30% for lifestyle and fun: Taking 30% of your earnings and allocating it to fund your lifestyle or hobbies and interests.

Why it's bullshit: Why a fixed amount based on a percent? This can either be limiting (not enough) or extravagant - too much. Later on in the book we will go into allocating and how to spend your money, and don't worry we will ensure your finances include making life good and having fun.

What about it works: If the amount needed to have a comfortable and fun life happened to work out to be exactly 30% then I guess it works out.

It takes money to make money: It has been said that you need to spend in order to earn.

Why it's bullshit: Spending money does not get you money. Money going out does not ensure money comes in. However, money can be used as a multiplier for volume of return and for speed, but it is not guaranteed. Making money comes down to application of the Economic Laws. Plenty have made money without spending a dime. Employees earn all their wages from their employer without themselves spending any money. It could be argued that they spend their time which is worth money - but to that I respond, "Says who?"

What about it works: Per Economic Law #10, putting money into something can speed up returns and amplify them (make them even bigger). When finding something that is successfully giving you a return, it would be wise to find out what part of that activity could give larger and faster returns if more money were put in.

You must go to college: There is an idea that attending college, and taking on large student loan debt to do so, is vital to living in the modern age. That without college you are less valuable, or it is harder to get a good job.

Why it's bullshit: The simple fact of attending college does not now make someone smarter or able to provide better goods or services. In most cases going to college requires taking on more debt than can be easily paid off. People often get student loans that they then are paying off for years to come. The typical time it takes someone to pay off a federal student loan is 20 years. College is often the expected and normal thing that people do. It has been preached for as long as colleges have existed. Going to college is the expected thing to do, but doing what is expected does not guarantee the outcome that is advertised. The higher education industry makes about $670 Billion per year. Further, according to a CNBC study in 2018, more than 40 percent of graduates do not get a job that requires a degree when they get out of college. And more than 20 percent still don't have a job that requires a degree after 10 years.

What about it works: College and continuing education provide valuable knowledge. This knowledge can give someone the skill necessary to develop or offer a supply that can meet market demands and so make money. Going to college or attending higher education for a specific trade or to learn a skill that can then be marketed and exchanged for money has definite value. However, a thing to remember is that most skills and abilities are taught for much lower costs online and a lot are even free to learn.

Be happy with what you have: This is how you should learn to be satisfied with your current lifestyle or quality of life and you shouldn't try to get more. Just settle for what you have now, don't reach higher.

Why it's bullshit: If you have to convince yourself that you are happy then you are not happy. Why not find the things that would make you happy that you don't yet have and get after them?

What about it works: Sometimes people forget to take a step back and see their current or recent accomplishments. This is important since only focusing on distant goals and how you aren't there yet could make someone unhappy. There are many milestones along the way and stopping for half a minute to admire an achievement, even if minor, is not a bad thing.

Spend 30% of your income on housing: It is instructed that you can afford 30% of whatever your total income is on your rent or mortgage. So, if you're earning $4,000 per month then you should spend about $1,200 on your housing.

Why it's bullshit: It's a blanket statement that determines how your quality of life should be. Some people can't afford 30% of their income on housing - and for some 30% is not enough to live in a decent place, depending on where they live. If an individual in San Francisco is making $75,000 a year, or $6,250 per month, then according to this formula they should spend $1,875 on housing. But a one-bedroom apartment in San Francisco goes for about $3,500. Obviously, the less that you have to spend on your housing the better.

What about it works: It's a simple formula for people to follow with little thinking involved. Also, spending more than 30% on rent or a mortgage leaves very little for other expenses.

Pay yourself first: This is the idea that you should ensure you give some of your income to yourself before sending it out on all the other expenses and bills.

Why it's bullshit: The government gets paid first. Taxes come out of your pay before it makes it to you in most cases. In the case of independent contractors, taxes get paid later, but taxes are unavoidable if you want to remain legal. If someone fails to give money to themselves, they aren't then chased by the government, but this is the case if you fail to pay your taxes. For most Americans, the leftover after the tax-man's cut is not enough to pay for the lifestyle they are living and also "pay themselves" in addition.

What about it works: If you set up your finances in such a way that there is no money left after paying debt, bills, and living expenses then that means you are paycheck to paycheck and will be unable to achieve financial stability. Putting aside money for yourself and your future before spending on living expenses can work for some, where discipline or an understanding of finances is lacking.

Pay yourself 10%: This ties in with paying yourself first. Often people who say pay yourself first also say the recommended amount is 10%.

Why it's bullshit: 10% could add up to a decent savings over a period of years. But in most cases, this is not enough to fund the desires or goals that people can have. Setting the amount at 10% makes the remaining 90% seem like it is supposed to be spent or even wasted. Why not determine what it is you want to fund and how fast you want to fund it, and then find out how much you need to allocate monthly to hit that goal - and then sticking to it.

What about it works: Setting up some sort of regular addition to a reserve, or savings is a smart idea. Adding to reserves is a necessary part of financial stability according to the Laws of Economics in Chapter 3.

You need to have a good credit score and do what you can to improve it: The idea is that your credit score is like some sort of social status. If you have a good score, then things will be easier for you and a lower score makes things hard.

Why it's bullshit: A credit score is no guarantee for a good quality of life - in fact it has much less impact on it in comparison to other aspects: such as income, expenses, savings, etc. Credit score only really comes up and has an impact in your life when getting loans or signing a lease agreement - the rest of the time it is just random arbitrary numbers that have no impact on your day to day living. Your credit score is not God.

What about it works: It inspires people to not take on stupid debt, or fund lifestyle with debt. This is good. Most things that add up to a decent or good credit score are basically smart financial decisions anyway. These smart financial decisions are good for improving your quality of life. Make smart financial decisions because it will improve your quality of life, not so you can have the highest credit score or bragging rights.

Measure your money in terms of hours worked: This idea is that you should think about your money as representing the number of hours it took you to earn it. For an hourly wage earner making $20 per hour, she would look at $100 as meaning 5 hours of work. She would see that spending $100 for a nice dinner and going out to the movies is equal to 5 hours of work. She would consider that night out as costing her 5 hours of time spent earlier, or 5 hours she would owe in the future.

Why it's bullshit: Time does not equal money, just as money does not equal time. Time becomes a point of complaint as most people cannot figure out how to make more money with the time they have in a week. This is because most people limit themselves to only 40 hours of income earning potential in a given week. It is at this point where time becomes a factor worth worrying about. The truth is: money is only reliant on time in the sense of the amount of time it takes to deliver a good or service in return for money. This "word of wisdom" can also be limiting in future planning as someone would only be looking at what they are able to have based on their available time. This is instead of figuring out other ways to generate the income to hit their goals. In other words, *"I can only get $800 from my 40 hours per week of*

61

work and so I will never be able to afford a vacation because I can't work more than 40 hours at my job."

What about it works: If someone is in debt and their debt keeps increasing, this can be a very valuable way to look at their money. Adding on another $100 for lifestyle expenses means another 5 hours of labor they would then be indebted to the Company Store (from the story of the coal miners in Chapter 5).

Get life insurance: Some people preach that life insurance is the best thing since sliced bread, and that not having a life insurance policy is irresponsible.

Why it's bullshit: Life insurance sounds much better than "A savings account that is accessible to those you leave when you die." But that is what it is. Life insurance is really not actually insurance. Death is inevitable. When you buy a life insurance policy you are betting that you will die within the term of the policy. If you bought a 20-year policy and die 21 years later, then there is no money. Remember you can't take your money with you when you die. You can only leave it for loved ones. Leaving some money behind is noble, but life insurance might not be the best option.

What about it works: Some policies can be cheap at only $20 or $30 per month. If things work out right, someone's loved ones could get half a million dollars when this person dies. BUT! It's not really a victory and it's not an investment. It's not even bittersweet, mostly just sad as a loved one died. For some people, if they're more concerned about the aftermath of their death or just unable to save, life insurance may give them some reassurance, but it isn't a substitute for good financial planning and decisions.

Get a small business loan: There is this idea that in order to get into business or start a small business, or even keep a small business going, you have to get a small business loan from the bank or government.

Why it's bullshit: There is definite value in having money to make necessary expenses to operate and get a business off the ground, but getting a loan is not the only way to do it. Getting a loan is like getting training wheels - it makes you feel safer and less at risk as you try to go faster than you are prepared for. Except the training wheels are not bolted on very tight and they have an expiration date. In this metaphor, the training wheels will fall off after a time and you could crash and get hurt, or you would need to get another set of training wheels (another loan).

What about it works: If 1) Someone identified an area of their business that was doing well and could expand rapidly if they invested some money into it. And 2) There was no other way to get the funds when they needed it: Then I can see the value in getting a small business loan. But a business should fund itself through its own efforts from the start, or at least very near the start. A small business that starts with a loan is beginning its existence already indebted to something else. Regardless if it's making any income or not it will still need to pay the debt.

Buy only the best deal or cheapest price: This is the idea that you should wait until you have found the cheapest price before making a purchase.

Why it's bullshit: Some people have waited far too long to make a deal and then lost earlier better deals as a result. I've seen people wait for the market price on certain electronics to go down only to have the next versions come out and make their waiting period start over. Save money? Yes! Don't buy things at inflated or crazy high prices where you can help it - but when you need an item, you need that item.

Find the best deal available at the time you need it and get the product and get on with your life.

What about it works: When there are two identical items, and one supplier is offering it at a discount over the other - then of course get the cheaper one. Buying items in bulk that are normally gone through at a rapid rate and for a discount is also a good idea.

Carry a balance on your credit card to build credit: There is an idea some have, that in order to increase their credit score they need to keep a balance on their credit cards.

Why it's bullshit: It is just not true. You do not need to keep a balance on your credit card to build up your credit score.

What about it works: It doesn't.

Get as much tax withholding as possible, get a bigger tax refund: Some people love to get those fat tax refunds at the end of the year. What a surprise it can be when you get a check in the mail from old Uncle Sam (the government) and now have some extra spending cash. The commercials on TV every year around that time start telling you all the cool things you can buy with this "extra money" from your tax refund.

Why it's bullshit: A tax refund *is* a refund. It's only a refund because you overpaid taxes during the year. This is money that was yours to begin with. Maximizing tax withholdings to increase your tax refund is only taking extra money out of your paycheck - you are reducing your take-home pay. Doing so to get a bigger refund is awful advice. You are giving up your money throughout the year and then if everything checks out you will get it back at the end.

What about it works: None of it - ideally you would end the tax year and get no refund and owe $0. This never happens, but if it could that would be the best scenario. Some might think they don't have discipline with their cash and so like the idea of using a tax refund as a sort of savings account. I would advise working on discipline instead, since overpaying taxes is not a solution to bad spending habits. Instead of relying on a tax refund, someone could stash the money instead.

Follow your passion and do what you love: Some preach that if you want to be successful, just follow what you are passionate about or make a business out of what you love.

Why it's bullshit: Just because something is your passion does not mean it is the passion of others. Sure, there will be other people who share it, but that does not mean that this is a market worth trying to offer a supply in - or that there is even a demand for it.

What about it works: Having enthusiasm for the things you do or the service you deliver is good! People should be passionate about delivering goods and services and about making money. Some people follow their passion and have tremendous success. Their success isn't due to following their passion though. Their success is from finding a demand, marketing their supply, and getting it delivered in return for money - See Economic Law #12. Sometimes this advice steers people away from the things that could have made them enough money to then be able to actually pursue their interests. I doubt there are many people whose passion is cleaning up the tragic sites of a murder scene - but for the professionals that do it, they *make a killing* (dark humor).

Wait __ amount of days or weeks before making a purchase: Some say it is a good idea to wait a certain amount of time like 24 hours or 7 days, or other lengths of time, before making a purchase to make sure you really want it before you actually pull the trigger and spend the money.

Why it's bullshit: When you are going to buy something, buy it. Waiting a random, or set, amount of days serves little purpose. The only thing you gain is the fact you waited - which is no added value, only wasted time. By the time most people want to buy something they have already shopped around (maybe even shopped around too much) and know what they want. When you know what you want, and there it is in front of you, and you have the money ready to buy it - don't wait. Snatch it up before someone else does or the deal changes.

What about it works: If you want to shop for other deals I can see waiting, but a set amount of time before a purchase is just silly - unless the purchaser has no self-restraint or discipline, and can only prevent bad spending by using weird control tactics like this one.

You have to give back: Big time business owners sometimes advertise how they give back and show off the times they "give back," as in giving things to their community. They sometimes preach that in order for you to be a worthwhile person you have to pay it forward.

Why it's bullshit: Giving back or donating is not a publicity stunt, but something people should do because it's needed and because of the value in supporting the community and the world. Helping others is always a good thing. However, in the formative stages of a business, or someone's wealth, there is little to give back - yet it's these people in the formative stages that this advice tends to be aimed at. Since most companies and startups operate without a profit, it doesn't make sense to be giving away more of the lifeblood of a company (the money) without first setting up a stable base. A stable base can then ensure actual and continual support for the community and charitable causes.

What about it works: Having worthwhile charitable causes to raise money for, and having something to contribute to is something I would consider a necessary part of living and business. Without it you can lose sight of yourself and your business. Having something to get behind and support gives you even more fire and drive and a lofty reason to seek increased profits and returns. Aligning a company with a worthwhile cause can also bring along employees and give them something they can contribute to that is worthy and bigger than themselves. The cumulative actions of many good people can influence major changes and shifts in the world - and more of it is needed if the world is going to get better, and if living conditions for all are to improve. I am a big supporter of charitable causes and drives. I have personally donated time and money far above and beyond what most people would consider massive contributions. Find a charitable cause and get behind it. Build your company and make profits so you can support it. With all that said, don't sacrifice your company to "give back" for a publicity stunt at the cost of your future ability to actually donate and donate well.

Spend money on experiences not things: I saw somewhere the advice to not buy something unless it would give you a memorable experience. The phrase sounds nice, but it also sounds like it belongs on a bumper sticker.

Why it's bullshit: It reinforces an inability to have or get things. It seems to say, "you are only allowed so much, and so spend your money where it counts."

What about it works: If you had to stretch your money and were only able buy things based on very limited choices, then I can see buying the things that are more memorable.

Simplify your accounts, have just one checking and one savings: Some people think it is too confusing to have more than one of each account type and so tell others to get rid of any additional accounts they may have.

Why it's bullshit: It doesn't make any sense that it would be easier to have fewer accounts. It just means there is less for you to think about or be responsible for. Having multiple accounts can actually make it easier as you can see at a glance exactly how much money is available in a particular account for a particular purpose without additional math. Splitting up money can make it easier to track funds for their allocated purposes and limit accidental loss or money slipping through the cracks. In a lot of business cases it makes sense to have multiple accounts even when it costs an extra account fee to do so.

What about it works: Multiple accounts in a small business start-up could simply mean you are paying additional account fees with no actual benefit. It really depends on the size of the business, the income level, and the complexity of the finances or allocations.

Just want less: People have preached that the best way to handle your desire to get more things, or the empty feeling some people have due to not owning the things they want, is to just change how they feel and want less.

Why it's bullshit: Do I need to explain this one? This is so silly. Make more money, kill wasteful expenses, get the things you want - it is your money. "Just want less" is a limiting factor that involves cutting yourself down to deal with disappointment instead of lifting yourself up.

What about it works: I guess if you were in prison this could be good advice.

Play it safe: Caution! Don't take risks! Be sure in what you do so you don't ever lose!

Why it's bullshit: Sometimes you need to jump. Playing it too safe cuts off the almost endless possibilities that are out there if you get out and take chances.

What about it works: Taking avoidable or unnecessary risks to seem cool or "smart" is just dumb. Potential risks should be weighed against potential rewards and decisions made with the recognition of the possibility of losing. Sometimes risks need to be taken. But yes, avoid the obviously dumb ones.

Work smarter, not harder: Don't work hard, work smarter. Lessen the amount of hard work you do by making the process easier and come be lazy with the rest of us.

Why it's bullshit: Developing a system to take over your workload is only half the equation. You need to work smarter AND harder. Massive smarts applied along with massive amounts of hard work and dedication multiplies the speed of success. If you find a way to simplify your process and use the extra time you freed up to expand your business or income instead of relaxing more, then you can build wealth even faster.

What about it works: Focusing on finding ways to simplify processes and make things smoother, faster, easier, and more profitable is always a good use of time.

Seek a balance of life and work: Slow down, take it easy. You've got to live your life some. Seek an equal balance of your work and your life. Live a little. Relax.

Why it's bullshit: The current economic systems in place in the world today are built around the promise of our ability to have some sort of balance. We try to find a way to balance out the amount of work we need to live and the time we have available for ourselves and family. Unfortunately, following that promise leads to ordinary lives. Very few people built massive wealth without lots of dedication and time spent working to pull it off. Do not forget about your family and obligations, but a true balance is just not feasible for most people in their current circumstances in today's world.

What about it works: You can't neglect the other parts of your life and just disappear into your business. You need to take care of yourself, your family, and the other parts too. These cannot be ignored without negative kick back or an eventual feeling of emptiness. Make time for these other parts of your life - they are important.

Don't make a plan, just go with the flow: Some people think plans are stupid and you should just be a leaf in the wind, going with the flow and seeing where it takes you.

Why it's bullshit: What a sorry excuse for failure. No plan means there is no course of action you have worked out to attain your desired goals - if you even have goals. Without goals and a plan to attain them how can you expect to get what you want or make much money? The wind is random - it blows quickly, slowly, east, west, north, south, up, down, in circles. It changes direction without notice and there is no predicting it. I would hate for my financial future to be like a leaf blowing in the wind, so I make plans. I revisit plans. I change them. I throw them out and make new ones, but I keep some course of action to get to my goals.

What about it works: You can blame "fate" or "bad luck" when things don't work out in your favor.

Pivot!: Sometimes I have heard aspiring entrepreneurs yell "Pivot!" much like Ross Geller in that episode of Friends. The one where they are moving the couch up the stairs in their New York apartment and get stuck in the corner of the stairs. Pivoting is when you realize your business is not gaining traction and another possible market-demand presents itself and so you change your business or product offering to meet this new demand.

Why it's bullshit: There are multiple factors that add up to a successful business - it is much more than just a hungry, demanding market standing in front of you begging for your product. There is a time and place for changing or adding an offering, but doing so just because some new direction looked more appealing at the moment can have a negative effect on the existing market or demand you were already meeting.

What about it works: Recognizing possible opportunities or new demands and taking action can sometimes be the difference between success and failure. This only comes about when: 1) the initial demand you thought you were supplying didn't exist or was mis-estimated, 2) your supply didn't actually fit the demand, 3) you never marketed or sold in the correct volume, or 4) you never generated want and then delivered with quality. See Economic Law #12. If you feel you need to pivot, I advise you find out which of these 4 points applies to your business and get that resolved as well.

Get feedback from your friends and family: This is normally the most readily available group of people that you can go bounce ideas off of and get their feedback on your product offering or service.

Why it's bullshit: Friends and family normally are not buying your product, and so what they say or think doesn't matter as much as those who will actually be the ones paying you money. Family and friends also might be sensitive to hurting your feelings and so not give honest feedback on what you are asking them about. The advice or feedback from a family member or friend could accidentally lead you in the wrong direction, away from meeting the demand of a market.

What about it works: Almost everyone has access to people who they can get a second or third opinion from about their ideas quickly and for free. But keep in mind, just because the opinions are given for free doesn't mean they're correct.

Focus on pain or pain points: This is about looking at what causes people pain and discomfort as a way to generate ideas or product offerings.

Why it's bullshit: Focusing on pain cuts the potential market by more than half. What about people's desires and wants, or the uplifting reasons for a purchase? Also, just because you built a business around someone else's pain does not mean they will buy it. See Economic Law #11: *If people do not know the existence of a good or service offering, they will not buy it - even if they are starving for it. If others are not made aware of your goods or services, they will not buy from you.*

What about it works: If someone doesn't like something then it is likely they will pay to get rid of it. Many people have built businesses and successfully expanded on this premise.

Seek outside capital or investors. Get funding: A surprisingly large number of start-ups have in their business plan to get outside funding from investors and venture capitalists. In most of these tech start-ups now-a-days, getting funding is listed on their business plan way, way before the part that involves ever making any income. What The F...

Why it's bullshit: Outside investment is not the determining factor of success in a company - even a tech startup. See again the Economic Laws in Chapter 3 if needed. Outside money can be used to quicken expansion, but it is far from guaranteed. And, giving up equity in your company is less desirable for you down the road. This can be quite a trade-off: more money now to get to the end faster, at the cost of not owning your whole company. This idea is often based on the business model of dumping the company and selling it off to someone else as fast as possible, rather than earning a profit from exchanging with customers in a market.

What about it works: It is sad to me how this is always seen as THE WAY and many start-ups think it's the only way to survive as a company in the modern age. Outside funding can help at times, such as a worthy investor who is personally interested in your success and helps in other ways besides just financially - or where an availability of cash allows the purchasing of something that will rocket the company forward.

Sell an unfinished product: Some have proposed the idea of not waiting for your product to be deliverable and to sell it in an unfinished state in order to get feedback from your customers that helps to shape the product for future sales.

Why it's bullshit: You can leave a bad taste in the mouth of your early customers. No one wants to buy an unfinished crappy product unless they have been heavily sold and possibly deceived. They don't get what they expected and so Economic Law #22 applies. They will want a refund, even if they don't ask for it.

What about it works: The idea of changing an offering or adding to it in order to continue to meet a demand or strengthen the demand is a sound principle, but not at the cost of wasting relationships with your early customers or adopters. Perhaps revealing an early prototype could be a great way to generate interest and future sales, but don't get tempted into promising something which you can't deliver. Not delivering what was sold will damage your future business and reputation.

Go easy on the marketing: There is an idea, sort of on the other extreme of "Sell an unfinished product." Which is to not pour the coals onto marketing. That your business ideas should be proofed thoroughly before investing into marketing.

Why it's bullshit: Sometimes people do a teeny, little bit of marketing, fail to get a result and then decide that it was a bad idea all along and toss it in the garbage can. Truth is, sometimes marketing needs a little bit of time to gain traction. Sometimes a marketing program is just a few days or weeks away from gaining the traction needed to have success. When a successful product with a demand is found, and a workable marketing campaign is worked out, then the coals should be poured on that program and fast.

What about it works: Intentionally crappy or dishonest business ideas should not be marketed just to see if they stick. Ideally, you are not using marketing and advertising to conduct market research. And marketing budgets should not be spent on unproven marketing tactics or campaigns.

Slow down, take your time and don't scale too fast: An idea went around for a while that it is best to have success slowly and not grow too fast. There is such a thing as growing too fast to easily handle the increased traffic, but only in the sense of not keeping up with it. The problem comes from not figuring out how to manage the sudden growth, not that the growth happened.

Why it's bullshit: We all want explosive growth and sudden expansion in our businesses and wealth. This "advice" cautions someone about achieving "too much success too fast." In the front of the mind of any business owner, or someone-seeking-wealth, should be how to have success and get it as rapidly as possible (Not by cheating or shortcutting, but by removing unnecessary obstacles and detours to arrive at the goal quicker.)

What about it works: If someone grows too quickly and is not prepared for it, then it can bite them in the ass and cause difficulties. An example would be a small company able to service 100 people at a time being promoted by a celebrity and suddenly having 1,000 people demanding service. Failing to deliver would upset these new customers. The problem here though is not the sudden growth, but the inability to adapt and think quickly to keep up with the sudden demand and then getting that demand met.

Be satisfied. Lower your expectations: Here is the idea of lowering your expectations and lessening goals so they are easier to hit. Some instruct to forget lofty goals and aim lower and then be satisfied with where you end up, partly on the basis that you can be happier with yourself since you at least accomplished something.

Why it's bullshit: If you don't aim high you won't hit high. I don't think there has ever been a success story of someone seeking to have a small, barely successful company and suddenly finding themselves in the Fortune 500. Often ideals change and higher goals get set and these lead to arriving at a higher level.

What about it works: I don't see any part of this idea that works.

Give employees whatever they want: Here is the idea that creating a friendly environment and a fully permissive workspace is what is desired. Give in to whatever employees want and let them have their way in hopes that they will like you more and hopefully produce more as a result.

Why it's bullshit: Business is not about winning a popularity contest. Business is about making money. This isn't meant to sound soulless, but if the focus is on making employees happy instead of earning income, then eventually there is less income to pay them, and then they will really be unhappy.

What about it works: Treating employees bad is a recipe for disaster. There needs to be an understanding displayed and compassion for the people who work for an employer. No one wants to work in a harsh or unpleasant environment, but people do want to get paid. Ensuring the company will survive and profits get made to adequately meet payroll and expand the company is first priority, next is the general well-being of the employees. Treat people nicely, but pay them first.

Cutting costs as the way to boost profit: Some people and businesses believe that if they cut corners, fire people, or make their product in a cheaper way they can increase profit by continuing to sell the product for the same price.

Why it's bullshit: People will notice and it can ruin a reputation. If something is going well, it is stupid to change it to try to squeeze out a few extra bucks. Cutting corners and delivering less than what's expected is a sure way to lose customers. Losing customers will cut into profits more than just about anything else that can affect earnings.

What about it works: Being wasteful in the production and delivery of goods and services is unwise. Finding ways to lessen the costs is not bad as long as it doesn't lessen the quality of the product or the quality of the business and employees that are delivering the product. Selling and delivering a product at a loss is very, very rarely a good idea since no company can survive long without making a profit (Economic Law #21.) Products that are losing money should be re-visited and re-worked so a profit can get made, even if not immediately.

Set realistic timelines: The idea that deadlines should be made easier to hit.

Why it's bullshit: "Realistic" timelines most often don't get hit either. This fits along the lines of lessening expectations. Timelines should be stiff and challenging, but not impossible. There is a point of making them actually real to attain, but not so easy that there is no challenge. Making timelines too easy for yourself lessens the number of things that can be accomplished with the available time.

What about it works: Insane and impossible timelines serve no purpose. A timeline set with no possible way to hit it only serves as a loss and a defeat. Setting yourself up for a defeat intentionally is not smart.

Be flexible: Be willing to adjust and give in on expectations or goals.

Why it's bullshit: Without persistence, most worthwhile goals don't get met. Often, we will be faced with opposition on the way to attaining wealth and business success. Being flexible on your goals (as long as they aren't insane) leads to a greater chance of your goals not getting met and slowing everything down.

What about it works: It is important to recognize changes as they occur and adjust to handle them so as to ensure the overall goals are met. But this is different from the idea of giving up on a goal once it gets a little difficult or pursuing something else that seems easier.

Seek resources for motivation or motivational content: Motivational writers and speakers tell you to go out and read books, listen to podcasts, watch YouTube videos, browse twitter feeds, scroll Facebook and Instagram posts for motivational content to get yourself motivated and pumped up.

Why it's bullshit: Motivational content is not a substitute for success. It can get someone off the couch and moving, but often the motivation is short lived. The person then comes back for more and ends up on a constant diet of motivational content, feeding themselves more and more and constantly trying to find the next nugget of motivation that will answer their problems and get them the success they are after. The need for motivational content normally then requires more motivational content to keep the person feeling motivated. I am mainly talking about the person reading their twenty-seventh book to get motivated and they still don't have anything substantial to show for it.

What about it works: It really can get people off their ass and moving, and this can have tremendous value. Sometimes this leads to true motivation: a worthwhile goal, the ability to stick to it, and inspiring achievements along the way.

Be confident: Some people say you just need to be confident. That being confident is the key to success and so... just... Be confident.

Why it's bullshit: Confidence isn't an on/off switch - so it is poor advice. It is like telling someone not to suck. Confidence is normally the result of familiarity and certainty in your skills or area of expertise. Having confidence and acting confident are not the same thing. Work with something more or spend more time with it if you want to feel more confident with whatever it is.

What about it works: Sometimes appearing confident can be inspiring or attractive to others.

It's all marketing. Don't worry about the product, just boost your marketing: This normally comes from the marketing wizard whose product is marketing systems, education, or a service. Sometimes this comes from the guy who has made his money ripping people off with a crappy or dishonest product. This is the idea that all you need in order to be successful is good and consistent marketing.

Why it's bullshit: No amount of marketing can make a dog turd something other than a dog turd. Marketing can make people think it is something other than what it is, but it cannot change the actual product. When that person shows up and finds out they were sold a dog turd they feel betrayed and will not buy from you again. This kills Economic Law #25 (previous customers) and cuts your future income off at the knees.

What about it works: Marketing is an incredibly important part of any business that must be granted the importance it deserves. You can't cut corners when it comes to properly marketing your product. Look again at the Laws of Economics in Chapter 3. Where a good product already exists and you are sure of it based on consistent customer feedback, your concentration should be on the creation and use of workable and effective marketing and sales campaigns.

Incorporate at the start of your business. Get your brand, website, etc.: A lot of places you might look for advice on starting-up-a-business recommend these things early on. Often the advice comes with affiliate links to companies that provide these services (Meaning they would earn money if you bought the service they recommended.) They tell you to go ahead and get a LLC set up, or some sort of corporation, get your ".com" bought and website built and also your branding, and go to town on your social media pages as well as setting up your email marketing newsletter service, and not to forget your logo design, also an accountant and your business bank accounts.

Why it's bullshit: None of those above things are actually required to make some money with a new business idea, yet most of them cost money.

What about it works: All of these things are needed - at a point. They are not the first things you need to get done when you start a new business, and these things should only come after getting a product developed and a demand identified. Now, different circumstances require different things of course, but advice to incorporate and spend money on legal fees when there is not even a product to build a business around is the wrong sequence. The start-up graveyard is filled with impressive looking incorporated companies along with their branded websites and social media profiles that never sold a product. Now, I'm not saying ignore or skip getting required licenses, etc. Always operate within the law or risk the consequence as per the economic law on following the rules (Law #19.)

Worry about the money later: This would be the idea of just going ahead living in idea-land or the beginning stages and don't try to make any money. That money will just come on its own at a later point if you keep at it. This is sort of like the phrase "build it and they will come" from the movie *Field of Dreams.*

Why it's bullshit: If money is not made to fund the business from the start, then it is impossible to fund the necessary business expenses unless you seek outside capital or go into debt. You could end up working for free a lot. Just because a nice product is developed doesn't mean people will show up to pay for it without any marketing - Economic Law #11.

What about it works: There is value in focusing on getting your name out there, but if you don't make money then you won't survive as a new company. Even with the best product in the world, if you can't afford to produce it, pay your staff, and market and deliver the product there won't be a company for long. Some truly excellent products never made it to market because no one had their attention on the financial survival of the company as a priority.

You can beat the market: You may have heard that with good investment advice you can beat the trends of current or future markets. This is meant as a motivation to keep investing even though there are signs indicating not to.

Why it's bullshit: A prediction in gambling is still gambling. You can assess and analyze and find things that are better bets than others, but investing in speculative returns is still gambling in the end. Someone's analysis might be inspirational and might seem promising, but following it is still taking a risk and could result in catastrophic loss.

What about it works: Outside of the stock market and speculative investing, I could appreciate the outlook of not feeling controlled or the effect of others in a marketplace. Finding ways to get ahead in business is necessary since pitfalls do show up.

You can't go wrong with real estate: Some say real estate is never a bad idea and investing in it is always safe to do. When the markets are at an all-time high you might hear this advice the most - but almost never at the bottom of the market. Interesting.

Why it's bullshit: This type of real estate investing is often speculative investing: putting money in with the hopes it will go up in value later, there are always risks of course.

What about it works: Just about every property bought can eventually be sold at a higher price later down the road, except in areas that have massive economic downturns, like parts of Detroit. Real estate still follows the Economic Laws, and the relative perceived value of properties goes up and down. There are also income producing properties which can definitely be good investments. Many people have made money flipping houses - a property is bought, fixed, and sold again for a profit. Flipping real estate is itself a business and if treated like a business can be successful.

Mortgage is good debt, or don't consider it as debt: I've heard people say that a mortgage is a good debt to have. I have also heard others say that when budgeting or analyzing debt, do not consider your mortgage as real debt. I believe this advice is offered because housing is a vital expense or because the debt is so large it will be being paid forever.

Why it's bullshit: This almost sounds like a sales gimmick from the lenders. Having a mortgage is still an indebtedness that requires your continued work to produce the income to pay it back or you lose your property! Mortgage agreements are made using the property itself as collateral, and so failing to pay it can get you kicked out and the property taken by the lender.

What about it works: Just about everyone will be paying monthly for housing. For this reason, it isn't sensible to look at your housing costs the same way you would look at a loan for a vacation. However, housing costs shouldn't be disregarded. The full weight of the loan and its obligations shouldn't be forgotten like the way many people disregard the weight of their student loans. In some instances, there can be tax advantages to a home mortgage which could be considered. Additionally, monthly payments on a mortgage establishes equity in the property over time.

Money can't buy happiness, or Money does buy happiness: Some have said money can't buy happiness meaning no matter how much money you have it can't make you happy. Others have said money does buy you happiness, if you just have enough, because then you can buy anything you want.

Why it's bullshit: Happiness has never been dependent on money. Happiness comes from other sources than material goods or wealth. The subject of happiness is not the point of this book. But simply having money, or not having any, does not determine if you are happy or not. However, not having money can lead to financial problems that add difficulty. Those difficulties can make things tough, so you might as well have as much money as possible.

What about it works: They are both kind of weird sayings, but there is some value in remembering that amassing money doesn't guarantee a worthy existence or a happy life as there are many other factors involved.

Diversify your portfolio and lower your risk: This is the belief that you should own some super safe, low-risk, low-return investments as well as some high-risk, high-return investments. That you should spread your investments into many different categories on the basis that losses in some will be made up by wins in others and it will sort of even out.

Why it's bullshit: Such investment recommendations are made by financial advisors, many of whom make their money from the amount of trades their clients make. Instead you could identify reliable sources of income and go all-in on making sure those work out. I am not talking about stocks, bonds, and other traditional investment instruments. I am talking about sources of income. Sources of income will be gone over in a later chapter.

What about it works: Pouring all your money into high-risk investments can lose you all of it in the long run. Pouring money into low-risk investments only will not return enough to make it worthwhile in the long run, unless it is a really, really long run.

Cut up your credit cards or freeze them in ice: I'm sure you've heard this one. This suggests that you have no self-restraint and the simple existence of a credit card in your home or wallet is enough to cause you excessive debt. That somehow the credit card remaining intact or not frozen in a block of ice will allow it to crawl its way onto your computer desk and into your online-store-of-choice and start making purchases.

Why it's bullshit: If you were such a maniac with an addiction to spending on credit, you wouldn't be reading this book. You would be somewhere charging up your cards on new purchases. Truth is, you can have 1 million dollars worth of credit available right next to you and guess what, it won't charge anything itself. If you have an understanding of the science of economics, then you will see credit for what it is. It's just credit, nothing more or less. It is not a monster and it is also not your god. It only causes a problem when not understood or not managed. And even then, it is the individual causing the trouble not the card.

What about it works: For some people the idea of having available credit that they can easily access acts as a crutch, giving them a false sense of security and can get in the way of their need to produce more income.

Have an emergency fund of 3 months' salary (or 6 months or 12 months): This is a very common piece of advice. That whatever your salary is you should have that amount multiplied by 3, 6, or 12 months.

Why it's bullshit: It isn't taking into account living expenses, and repayment of debt. It isn't about getting an amount of money that is allocated for a specific purpose, but just an arbitrary amount of money that sounds nice and allows for easy math for people. Ideally, you would have considerably more than this saved up and you would have different funds allocated for different purposes. You should have enough to cover emergencies, and it should never get tapped into because you would never allow yourself to go 12 months, or however long, without income.

What about it works: It is an easily repeatable saying that gets people to look at the need to have some money stashed for emergencies. This is a good thing. Having a reserve and adding to it is a must. The unfortunate thing about this saying is it can actually limit how much money is stashed once the suggested 1, 3, 6, or 12 months' salary figure is hit.

Automate your budget, get an app to do it for you: Apps have been developed that keep track of your spending and tell you how much money you have available at any point in the month. These apps tell you how much money you are allowed to spend in the categories you set up.

Why it's bullshit: Let's say it is lunch time and your app says your remaining food budget is $5.00. This doesn't allow for much of a lunch these days and you can't just skip eating, so you will probably have to break the budget anyway. Don't use an app to tell you what you can or can't spend based on someone else's judgement of what is a "smart budget." It's better to be an active part of your own financial decisions. Don't have your phone make choices for you and determine how you are going to live. Instead, get a rock-solid understanding of your finances and the science of economics and use it. You don't have to be the effect of your money.

Learn to handle your money so it doesn't handle you.

What about it works: If someone is unwilling to ever learn about finances then I can see how using an app could partially help with limiting unknown and/or wasteful spending. Then at least the person should be able to have food and shelter.

Money is the root of all evil: We've all heard this one. That money motivates evil and that all evil stems from an interest in gaining more money.

Why it's bullshit: Evil people do evil things regardless if there is money involved or not. A certain amount of people in the world are just plain evil, but luckily it isn't a very large amount. Evil people who want to hurt others are not in it for some imagined payday. Visit a prison or insane asylum, talk to the rapists and murderers, and find out: did they commit their crimes with the belief someone would pay them? I'll save you from a horrifying trip: the answer is *no*.

What about it works: Sometimes weak people can be bribed or manipulated into committing evil deeds with the promise of money. Most corporate sabotage or spying is done for the promise of payment. There are lawyers who get paid every day to help unmistakably guilty criminals get off the hook for crimes they obviously committed. They do this for personal financial gain, not for some sense of justice. There is some truth that people do evil for pay, but money itself is not the cause of evil.

Time is money: Here we have the idea that either time is itself a currency, or that time is the same as money. Some say that you should look at time in the same way you look at money, or that you should look at your money as a representation of time spent.

Why it's bullshit: Time is not dependent on money and vice-versa. However, the effective use of time can accelerate and increase income potential. Time itself is not the primary factor in making money. There are those who spend 40 hours to earn $400, and there are those who earn $35,000 in the same 40 hours. The takeaway here is that with a thorough understanding and application of economics, someone's income doesn't need to be tied to time.

What about it works: It is most often said with the implied meaning of "hurry the hell up." This can be a valuable way to go about business activities since the faster you can complete something, the faster you can deliver. The faster you deliver, the more you can sell, and the more you can get paid, and so on. It's true that there is only so much time in a week, specifically there are 168 hours - no more and no less. Time is a necessary component in most cases to making money and so time shouldn't be wasted and should be treated as a resource.

A penny saved is a penny earned, or a dollar saved is a dollar earned: This saying means that any money someone manages to not spend is equal to money they earned. That finding ways to not spend money means you will have more.

Why it's bullshit: Per Economic Law #10, money finds a way to get spent, even if it takes a while. Businesses and people tend to find a way to spend more than they earn - if not today, then eventually. Things come up requiring more money than was planned for and so the savings get used. Saving money does not have the same importance as earning it. But adding to savings is important and is a part of the formula for financial security from Economic Law #24.

What about it works: Too many people do not see the importance of keeping some of the money they earn and so keep a near 1:1 ratio of money-in to money-out. For example: $4,000 in income and $3950 in expenses for the same time period. Finding ways to keep money is important. Finding ways to increase income is more important. And, keeping some of what you get is necessary for your future.

Don't invest if you are in debt: Some people have said it's unsmart to make investments without first paying off all your debt and that paying off debt should be the first priority.

Why it's bullshit: There are many different circumstances and opportunities in life. We will be going over debts and investments in more detail later, and from those chapters you will see when to use debt and when to make investments, as well as how. But simply following the rule of paying debt before investments without looking at what is available can shut you off from opportunities.

What about it works: Carrying a credit card debt of $10,000 with an 18% interest rate means you will be paying $1,800 in interest during the first year. If at the same time you invested $10,000 at the desirable stock market rate of 8%, that would pay you $800 per year. The difference between the investment and the debt results in a $1,000 loss. In similar circumstances it would be wise to pay off credit card debt first, especially when comparing debt to stocks or speculative investments. The interest rate on debt is guaranteed, whereas returns on investments are often not. So, if there is available cash it would probably be best to pay off high interest debt first, but you will need to assess each situation.

Summary:

The main point in going over all of these "words of wisdom" is: following the commonly repeated advice or conventional "wisdom," though it sounds good and sounds like it is the right thing or what you are supposed to do, often leads people to a place where they don't want to be. You probably have already seen or experienced it or at least understand this to be true. The purpose of this book is not to lead you to an average life with average finances, but help you achieve your goals.

So now you might ask, *"Then what do I do with my money? How do I gain wealth? How do I get where I want to be? How do I get the things I want?"*

Factually, these questions are answered for the most part in the Laws of Economics from Chapter 3. But we will be breaking things down into more detail and you will be gaining a greater understanding in the following chapters.

CHAPTER 7: WHAT MONEY IS & HOW MONEY WORKS

Some historians believe that the earliest use and development of money comes from a place called Mesopotamia about 5,000 years ago. Other historians acknowledge the strong possibility of some form of currency being used as far back as 40,000 years.

Whatever the origin of money may be, it was created and used for one reason: to make it easier to trade things of value.

Let's look again at the definition of money from Chapter 1. MONEY: Something that represents value and can be given in return for something else considered of value. Money is a representation of all the things the people in a society consider valuable. They have trust that its value will stay true and be upheld by others. If they don't trust it, it loses value. Different cultures and civilizations have used different currencies or forms of money over time, but it all boils down to something to represent other things of value, such as hours worked is worth X amount of money, or a new TV is worth X amount, or a new house is valued at X.

To help explain this we have a little story. Story time:

If you were a farmer thousands of years ago that exclusively grew fruit and became hungry for something else, there would have only been a few options available to you. Let's say you wanted some meat. You could go hunting, you could steal some from somebody else, or you could trade for it.

If you had no hunting skills, and you didn't want to steal someone else's meat for fear of getting caught and maybe killed, then you would have only one real option. You would need to trade for it.

You would have to go to your neighbors and try to trade some of your fruit. You would have to hope they wanted some of what you had to offer. What if they didn't want your fruit? Then hopefully you could trade some labor, or some other available resource.

If your neighbor, the cow farmer with spare meat, was interested in your fruit - then perfect, but he would probably want to see it first before striking a deal. For this reason, you might have had to travel with a large supply of fruit to show. This could be bulky and troublesome.

What if your neighbor wasn't interested? You would then need to find something else of interest to him or travel further with your bulky supply and try other farmers to see if they were interested.

Let's say, to make this story easy, your neighbor takes you up on the offer and gives you some meat in return for your fruit. You two discuss the arrangements for a while and then come to an agreement. He gets more of your fruit than you think is fair, but since you approached him and wanted some of his supply you agree to the trade.

You go back home and enjoy your meat. The next day you are thirsty. But you don't want water, you want some wine. Now, you have some fruit, a little left-over meat, and the ability to provide some labor. Now it's time to find someone with wine who would trade for something you can offer.

You travel around bringing your bulky supply with you. You finally get to someone with some wine, but he isn't interested in your offerings. He is only interested in some wool, and you don't have any.

Determined, you set off to find out what the sheep farmer wants in return for some wool...

Looking at this little story we can already see economics at work - the Laws in application. The absence of money definitely slows down trade doesn't it?

Somewhere along this society's development, someone introduces the concept of money. The king gets busy manufacturing and distributing it. Money coming into the picture allows you, the fruit farmer, to sell your fruit for money and then using this money buy each of the things that you want for an agreed upon price and be done with it. No more dragging your bulky fruit supply around with you, and no more going in circles trying to get what you want.

Money also simplifies the collecting of taxes by the king and government. Since all of the work and goods sold are converted into the same desirable object (money), it is much easier for the king's men or tax agents to swing by and take their slice of the pie.

We see that money is what is gotten in return for the sale of your goods and services, and also what is used to purchase the goods or services you want.

Now, what happens if the king gets carried away and makes five times as much money as was previously in circulation? The king, who controls the creation and distribution of the currency, figures that if he makes even more money and puts it out into the community, then the common people will trade more and he can collect more in taxes. He concludes this will make him even richer. Suddenly this little community of farmers goes from having 100 money units in circulation to over 500.

You, the fruit farmer, find you now have more money. You now have 85 units of money where you used to have around 20. There is now more money going around and more people coming to buy fruit. You decide you are going to get some more meat and so head to the cow farmer and ask to get 40 money units worth. You were expecting a much larger portion than he gives you. He gives you only slightly more than what you consider is 10 units worth.

Outraged, you demand answers. He explains that people have been showing up with more money and wanting to buy more meat at a time. But he hasn't had any increase in meat supply to offer. He has the same amount of meat as he did before, but suddenly the people are now showing up with five times the amount of money and wanting to buy more meat than ever before. He had to raise prices, or he'd be completely sold out. Since he raised his prices, he didn't empty out his supply to the first two buyers who came by with their increased money units. He explains as a result of the increase in price there is some left over and that you can still buy some - it just costs you more. You give up arguing and buy the meat at the increased price since you still want it. As you walk away you decide it must be time to raise the price of your fruit so you can afford the higher price of meat.

This is inflation.

When the king comes around you pay the increased taxes. You still don't have any more fruit then you had before - your farm didn't get any bigger and the plants didn't start producing more fruit.

The other farmers in the community don't like it either, but they deal with it. Someone comes along and announces himself as a money expert. His name is Mr. Banker. He goes on to tell everyone that inflation should be expected and that it is natural. You and the other farmers should expect a certain percentage of inflation to continue every year. You all figure that since you are just farmers and he is the expert on money, he must know what he's talking about and should be trusted. So, people give in and agree to the idea of inflation being natural, or they forget about it all together.

At some point the king goes to war and has to hire mercenaries from another kingdom. The king gathers as much money as he can to pay for this war and the total amount of money in circulation reduces significantly. The war is won, but most of the money has left the community and its small economy.

For those in the community that still have some money, they now see an increased value in it. Money can buy more than it did before since there is less available money in comparison to the available things to buy. You go back to the meat farmer and find that no one is buying meat anymore. Nobody wants to spend what little money they have on meat. Because of this he had to cut his prices, and an amount of meat that would have cost 10 units before the war now only costs 2.

This is deflation.

The king needs more money. He might have to go to war again. He sees things in his land that he needs to upgrade or fix, such as road conditions or the waterways, etc. He doesn't want to part with the money he keeps in his vault, so he figures if he creates more units of money, sends it out, and then collects it in taxes, he will be able to use that new money to pay for the things he needs. And so, he makes more money. To cover up the fact that he is just printing off more money, the king thinks of ways to get it introduced into the community without the citizens fully realizing what is happening.

The king finds handouts and charitable contributions for the new money. He makes "loans" for which he doesn't require repayment, or very little repayment. He finds people who are in need of healthcare and can't afford it and provides funding for that. He finds hungry people and sponsors a program to feed the hungry. He also uses money to pay employees to manage these programs and funds services to help the community. Interestingly enough, he also requires taxes from the employees he pays to manage his programs.

You, the fruit farmer, find that you are requiring more and more money in order to buy the things you want, but your farm is the same size. You aren't producing any more fruit in order to keep up with the ever-increasing cost of goods and services. The things you want to have keep costing more and more. You also want other things now besides just wine and meat. You see your neighbors with their improved homes and nice pets, and you want these things too. You never ask how they got them and so just assume you are inadequate or less fortunate.

One day the nice money expert from earlier appears. He introduces himself to you as Mr. Banker. He is a cousin to the king, but never mind that fact. He is here to let you know he helps the community, and he can help you.

He helped the meat farmer with a loan. The meat farmer used the loan to purchase more cattle and then he was able to sell more meat. And with the increased sales he now has more money than ever before. You remember how successful the meat farmer looks and so you ask if you can get a loan too. He smiles. You do the math and ask for enough to pay for doubling the size of your farm. Mr. Banker needs to do an analysis first to see if you qualify. He walks your farm and property and after some thinking offers you a deal. He offers you enough money for you to increase the size of your farm by half. Not double as you had asked, but you are approved and so you feel obligated to take it. You think about all the success other people are having and how Mr. Banker must be the reason for everyone's success. You want some success for yourself, so you stick out your hand to shake on it.

He tells you there are some terms to the loan. He shakes your hand as he explains the terms. You are obligated to give him 2% of your monthly crops or its equivalent in money. This is in addition to the monthly payments that go towards paying off the loan. You need to eventually pay back the full amount of money he gives you. If you are late on a payment, there is an additional fee. If you fail to make payments enough times he will come and take your whole farm away from you and the king and king's guards will help him do it. You smile nervously but figure everyone is doing this so it must be safe.

You fail to do the math to see that you will be paying him back 3X the original loan amount, and that the increased size of your farm isn't enough for you to produce the level of income you actually need in order to make everything work. You fail to see that even with this loan, you will not have enough money to create the impact you were hoping for. You fail to really understand what collateral is, that your farm is held as a fail-safe. You miss the point that if you fail to pay, he can take your farm from you to "make up his loss."

A few days later he comes back to give you your loan. He drops off a bag full of money! You start thinking about all the things you always wanted but were never able to afford. You think about all the things you could buy instead of upgrading your farm if you wanted to. You think that this might be the most money you have ever seen at one time.

You get back on track and you use it to fund your improvements. You buy a little more land on the edge of your property and begin to expand your farm. At the end of the first month Mr. Banker shows up right on time and is ready for his monthly payment AND his 2% of your crop. You pay him so he will leave you alone and you get to forget about him for the time being - at least another month.

You pay others to get your new land ready to plant more seeds. After a few months, and a few more payments on the loan, the money is all used up. Your farm is 50% bigger than it was before, and you are happy for it.

Another month comes around and you aren't selling any more crops than the months before. The rest of the people in the community don't know you have more fruit to sell. Maybe some of them do, but they don't have an increased desire or at least don't want more than they were already getting (remember the Economic Laws on demand). Also, Mr. Banker gave loans to other members of the community and their monthly payment obligations reduced their available money for goods and services. You didn't sell anymore this month than the last month, but you have an increased expense to maintain your larger farm.

Mr. Banker comes around and is ready to collect his monthly payment and his 2% of the crop. You tell him you can't afford it and that you don't have it ready since your monthly expenses increased to deal with the extra required maintenance. He reminds you that you made a deal and walks off.

You are now stressed out. How are you going to pull all this off?

The next month rolls around and you now owe 2% of the crop again and another payment on top of last month's missed payment. Additionally, there is a late fee on top of all that. Mr. Banker comes by and reminds you about your deal but doesn't seem too upset that you still aren't paying him. He knows what's coming.

You start to think that maybe if you got another loan then you could use the second loan to pay off the first loan. Maybe you can use a second loan to make your farm bigger or pay for some marketing or something.

To keep this story from going on and on we won't continue down this typical storyline of getting a second loan to try to stay alive.

Eventually Mr. Banker comes by and explains that since you have missed a certain number of payments, he now owns your farm. You have 100 days to leave or the king's guard will show up and force you out.

"This is unfair!" you scream, "I built this farm from nothing!" Mr. Banker reminds you that you made a deal. He smiles.

At the end of 100 days you sadly leave your farm. Mr. Banker collects the property and after a very short time sells it off to one of his close associates. Now someone else owns the farm. This new owner also gets all the upgrades and increased expansion you put into it.

You go off and find a job as a laborer on someone else's farm.

You work hard and save up some money over the years.

Down the road money isn't worth what it was when you were younger and had your own farm, but eventually you save up enough to purchase a farm one tenth the size of the one you had before.

You plant some fruit and get a small crop going. You learn about these things called investments where you can purchase a small piece of someone else's farm. You never get to take any of their crops, but you "own" a piece of it. Mr. Banker helps you out with buying some of these pieces. You can only buy them through him since he is the broker, of course there is a small fee attached to each one. You buy these hoping that at some point later you can sell them for more than the price you paid for them.

Eventually you die and leave your small farm, your "pieces of other people's farms", and a small amount of money to your children. By the time they get around to selling the assets, they make more than what you spent when you bought it all. They make a decent chunk of money and try to move on. They can't particularly be happy about this money because they got this inheritance at the cost of losing a loved one.

The End.

Sounds grim huh? It's a sad story that is repeated all too often. There was a little extra here on a forming community and money system, but the loans and loss happens in our current society all the time. As touched on multiple points earlier, almost everyone you meet carries more debt than they could reasonably hope to pay off in several years.

CHAPTER 8: HOW TO SPEND MONEY – WHAT THINGS YOU SHOULD BE SPENDING YOUR MONEY ON

We are going to go over how you can use your money. I'm not offering a system or something automatic that makes choices for you. The goal is not to remove your financial responsibility, where you just plug in percentages here and some money there and not think about where your money is going.

Instead I am offering you an understanding on this subject, along with some guidance, so you can consciously and intentionally put your money in the right direction.

To kick off this chapter I want to remind you again of the first step in losing on the subject of finances out of Chapter 5:

The first step in losing the economic battle is by being convinced you need more than you have in order to live.

When people believe they need more than they have in order to live, they will feel obligated to keep spending. By spending on more than the things they need to live, the amount of money that they are required to have goes up.

NECESSITY: Something that you cannot do without. You have to have it in order to continue living. Some examples include food, shelter, water, and more. I would argue that a cell phone is a necessity. You might argue that coffee is a necessity - I don't see a problem with that. In a business sense, necessities would include things like rent, marketing expenses, as well as money to pay employees and basic things needed to operate.

The first thing to spend money on: Necessities. I don't think I need to explain how to spend money on necessities, you just do so. The quality or price of the necessity is of lesser importance than ensuring you have it. Some people like expensive coffee and some people like cheap coffee. Take your pick, but do you *need* it? The $10 latte might be nice, but do you *need* it? Evaluate that before counting it as a necessity. A very important point on necessities, especially as applied to business: Necessities would include the things that are required in order to produce future money. This is not investments, but things like supplies, phone, internet, etc. These things are almost as important as food because without the supplies required to make more money, you won't be able to make more money.

You need to decide what are necessities for you, not me. I won't list off the reasons why a $10 coffee every day is stupid, since for you it might not be stupid. For some people, a car is a necessity and for others it might not be.

I know that most of the time when someone is reading a book and the author tells the reader to grab a pen and note things down or do an exercise, they don't. Fine. But grab your phone, open a notepad, and list out your necessities.

List out all the things you actually need to have in order to live and how much they cost you monthly. Example:

Necessities:
Housing & Utilities + Internet- $1,850
Phone: $50
Food & Coffee - roughly $450
Car payment - $250
Car insurance - $100

Gas: $300
Total: $3000

Now we know how much money you need to spend each month just to be alive. This is your cost of living. Notice how repayment of loans is not included in this and neither is investments or a retirement plan.

In this above example if you obtain less than $3000 in cash each month, then you can't even afford to live, or at least live as your life is currently set up.

With basic math you see there are two options here: Make more money or lessen the cost of living.

How to lessen the cost of living?

1. Identify things mistakenly classified as needed in order to live and remove them.
2. Find cheaper alternatives to the necessities you are buying.

How do you make more money? By understanding and applying the Laws of Economics, more specifically Laws #12 and #27.

I really urge you to take a break in reading and work this out for yourself. Really work this out and then answer this question:

Can you afford to live your life?

If this is not a yes, then do the above (lessen expenses, or find ways to increase income) until it is a yes.

Once you have a yes then we can carry on with the rest of this chapter.

Seriously, do it.

Did you do it? Did you just say yes? Well, you didn't fool me! Go and find out if you can afford your life and then I will carry on. Go. Do it quickly. I'll wait here.

Okay, done? Carrying on.

Notice that debt was not included in your cost of living - this is because it isn't a necessity. It is not on the same level as housing, food, or things required to produce more income.

In order to better break down what to spend money on, we will look at the different steps in losing the economic battle. It's obvious that not understanding the Laws and basics of economics is the main cause of losing, so I'm not listing that out specifically. Besides not understanding the Economic Laws, these are the five main factors in losing at the financial part of life:

The first step in losing the economic battle is: **1) Being convinced you need more than you have in order to live.**

We've talked about this point a few times before. By being convinced you need more than you have, you then feel an urgency and a being-pulled-feeling to buy more than you can. This then causes your expenses to go up. You find your money draining away to pay for the things that you feel you need or were at least convinced you needed. This also opens the door to using debt to fund lifestyle. Too many people go into debt because of this point, and this is the main cause of most people's debts today.

The second step in losing the battle of economics is: **2) Not consistently allocating money for future income producing methods, and not considering this a necessity.**

After you have your basic cost of living figured out and covered, if you don't also allocate money for future income producing methods then there are less choices for increasing your level of income. This can then lead to a sort of continuous repeat month after month. If creating future income is not allocated for, then future debt is almost guaranteed. Money saved does not mean that it won't get spent. Emergencies happen and unexpected things occur that drain your savings. Without increasing income, your savings don't get replenished or you end up having to rely on debt.

The third step is: **3) Not having and maintaining a reserve or reserves for future potential needs or opportunities.**

Too many people live paycheck to paycheck. The first cause of this is the first reason for losing the battle, the second cause is the 2nd, and this one here is the third. People plan to get married and save for a future wedding, some people save for their kids to use towards college tuitions, and some save for a down payment on a house.

Few people have worked out how much money they would need to live if they found themselves unable to work for a month and keep that amount locked up in the vault.

Fewer people have a fund set aside for future potential upgrades to their house. As a result, when they come around to seeing they need improvements it requires a loan. They often use the house as collateral to get such loans.

Even fewer people collect a pool of cash to have on hand should they find themselves face to face with a deal or opportunity too good to pass up, such as a great income producing investment.

The point I'm making here is not "having enough money saved for when you need it," but finding out for yourself: what are the future things you want to fund or be prepared for, and then starting specific reserves for each specific thing and adding money to these reserves regularly.

Failing on this point is another factor that pushes people further into debt.

Fourth: **4) Not having a workable way to handle debt and obligations.**

Debt is almost a sure thing for almost everyone at some point in their life.

Not having a plan or way to get out of the debt ensures continual payments and enslavement to *The Company Store* (coal miner story from chapter 5).

For the most security, when debt is used it should be used with a plan of how it will be gotten rid of and when.

Unfortunately, there are too many people who are in debt and don't think about or understand the full weight of their debt, in addition to the monthly payments. They then go on happily making monthly payments forever. They look at a new car as $350 per month - easy! They can afford another $350 a month, or knock something off to make room for that payment. They don't look at the actual cost of things, like for the car the actual cost is $33,600 over 8 years plus another legally binding contract that they can't walk away from.

Unfortunately, most people don't even target the paying off of their debt until they have some sort of awakening moment. The sad thing is that at that point things are normally collapsing and caving in on them. They then resort to firm and stable decisions and follow along some system presented to them, still lacking a workable understanding on the subject of finances.

The fifth step in losing, and probably the biggest and most harmful one of them all: **5) Making a budget based on income and using a level of income to determine expenses, rather than getting the level of income up to necessary spending levels.**

There were several bullshit "words of wisdom" in Chapter 6 along these lines. Things like: 30% of income to housing, 10% to yourself, 30% to fun and hobbies, etc.

Budgeting based on your income doesn't lift you up - it doesn't improve your life. It only brings you down!

You have to come down to "the level you're at" in order to live. This one is the saddest for me to see, and it brings about a continuing decline for people. Since the budget is affected by the income, what if the income goes down?

When the income goes down then you immediately have to give up more things - even more sad. Since the income is less and the budget is based on the available income, then when income is less the budget is less. This requires you to make sacrifices.

To make it even worse, what happens when your income goes up? Almost every single person out there makes the mistake of increasing their budget now - more income means more money to spend on housing, fun, etc. Yes, it is true there is more money to spend – 30% dedicated for housing on $100,000 is much more than 30% of $60,000. People follow their budgets as instructed, and by doing so their expenses increase to match. This then makes it so they do not attain financial security.

This is why there are people who make 6 or 7 figures ($100,000 or $1,000,000) a year and are in monster debt, feel broke, and under constant stress.

To say it again: People don't make their budgets based on what they want to have, but instead based on what they feel they are allowed to have with their current level of income.

Budgets based on income in combination with feeling like they need more than they have in order to live is an almost guarantee for never-ending debt.

This also might just be the most promoted piece of advice out there: make a budget. Having an idea of your expenses is very important! I asked you to do that at the beginning of this chapter, but I didn't ask you to figure out what lifestyle you can afford based on your income. I asked you to figure out how much it costs you to live. In a little bit I will ask you how much it costs to get what you want.

If you have been on a defense-based-budgeting lifestyle, of changing expenses based on your income, then I hope this serves as the turning point for you in your life.

The winning way is just a few pages ahead - you are almost there.

If we take these losing points, where people lose at the battle of economics and reverse them, we see the winning way. This is the winning way to *use* your money:

1. **Have an understanding of what it costs you to live and produce more income than what is needed to be alive.**

2. Allocate for future income producing needs, consider having money for future income-producing purchases a necessity.
3. Have reserves set up to fund future opportunities or potential needs.
4. Have a plan to address debt and stick to it. Don't incur debt without a plan for handling it as well.
5. Factor in all things that you need and desire to spend money on - EVERYTHING. Use this amount as your budget and then work to get your income to that level and above. Don't budget in reaction to income, but instead plan how to spend your money before you make it.

These are also presented in order of importance. Point one needs to be addressed before point two, and two before three and so on.

Let's dive in a bit and go over some ways to use these 5 winning factors.

One: Have an understanding of what it costs you to live and produce more income than what is needed to be alive.

This was addressed earlier at the beginning of the chapter. I am going to copy-paste it here to save you the trouble of flipping back on this one:

List out all the things you actually need to have in order to live and how much they cost you monthly. Example:

Necessities:
Housing & Utilities + Internet- $1,850
Phone: $50
Food & Coffee - roughly $450
Car payment - $250

Car insurance - $100
Gas: $300
Total: $3000

Now we know how much money you need to spend each month just to be alive. This is your cost of living. Notice how repayment of loans is not included in this and neither is investments or a retirement plan.

In this above example if you obtain less than $3000 in cash each month, then you can't even afford to live, or at least live as your life is currently set up.

With basic math you see there are two options here: Make more money or lessen the cost of living.

How to lessen the cost of living?

1. Identify things mistakenly classified as needed in order to live and remove them.
2. Find cheaper alternatives to the necessities you are buying.

How do you make more money? By understanding and applying the Laws of Economics, more specifically Laws #12 and #27.

I really urge you to take a break in reading and work this out for yourself. Really work this out and then answer this question:

Can you afford to live your life?

If this is not a yes, then do the above (lessen expenses, or find ways to increase income) until it is a yes.

Two: Allocate for future income producing needs, consider having money for future income-producing purchases a necessity.

In addition to paying for the cost of living you need to pay for things that will make you more money or allow you to make more money.

Here are some examples of things that allow you to make more money or help you because they might be necessary in producing income. Some of these might already be listed as necessities for you depending on your source or sources of income:

- Cell phone
- Internet
- Paper and pens
- Postage
- Computer and computer repairs/upgrades
- Work/office space or workshop
- Employees
- Inventory to sell
- Tools
- Machinery & maintenance
- Advertising
- Etc.

Here are some examples of things that would help make you more money. These differ from the above as they are not a regular expense that permits income, but some examples of things that would enable you to increase your income in the future:

- Market research
- Things to upgrade quality of product
- New hires
- Consulting or coaching
- Studies and learning
- Upgrades of brand and brand image

- Public relation activities
- Etc.

When you get money in, some portion of it should be used to pay for things that will increase your income in the future.

Three: Have reserves set up to fund specific future opportunities or potential needs.

This is different from just having a savings account or extra cash available. This is working out what you want to fund and then slowly (or quickly) adding money to an account for that purpose on a regular basis.

This will reduce the need to rely on debt. Doing so gives you the needed funds down the road and opens the possibility to purchase things with cash, or mostly with cash.

This also gives you money to invest in income producing things should you find opportunities. An opportunity is a situation or change in something that makes it possible for you to do something you want to do or attain a goal. Specifically, I'm talking about opportunities to make more money.

"What opportunities?" you ask? Well they are there. They do exist and they do come across your path. You might not notice them because you are looking the other way. I am not criticizing you. I'm just pointing out that if you aren't thinking about having money to fund an opportunity then you're probably not noticing them. You wouldn't be able to do anything with opportunities requiring money if you didn't have any, so why would they grab your attention?

Finding an opportunity is secondary to the importance of having some funds available to finance one. In fact, I would advise having a special reserve fund that you call *The*

Opportunity Fund, which just collects money until you find an opportunity you want to fund.

Now, besides future income opportunities we also have other potential needs that will require funding. These are things like emergencies, vacations, home improvement, car upgrades, future studies, donations, charitable contributions, etc. I am not saying you need a reserve fund for each of those categories, but you do need reserves for the things that you want or think you will need later.

This comes before debt in the sequence of working out your spending because having the funds, or some funds available, is what removes the need to use debt. If you had worked out the things you wanted in the past before you had to have them, and had funds or reserves for those specific things, then you wouldn't have needed to rely on debt to get them in the first place.

If you don't have some funds or reserves set up now and only focus on debt, then when the debt is paid off and you want something else or have an emergency, you will need to rely on debt again.

Four: Have a plan to address debt and stick to it. Don't incur debt without a plan for handling it as well.

There is an upcoming chapter about debt and getting out of debt, so I will be brief here: when taking on a purchase using debt, do the math to see how you will pay it off, how long it will take, and how much you will pay in the long run. Do the math as a minimum before incurring the debt. If you do this each time you consider adding debt, you might find yourself taking on much less debt than before.

The time to plan how to repay a debt is before incurring it, not after you are overwhelmed by it.

Five: Factor in all things that you need and desire to spend money on - EVERYTHING. Use this amount as your budget and then work to get your income to that level and above. Don't budget in reaction to income, but instead plan how to spend your money before you make it.

Doing these steps will help you get the things you want and help you not end up with things you don't want or didn't plan for. Increasing your budget in relation to increased income, as discussed earlier, is a recipe for collecting more and more stuff whether you truly want it or not.

Step Five is easy to do, just go back through the earlier steps with your pen and paper, or your phone's notepad app open, and write down all the things you need, want, and want in the future and how much they cost. Take the time, write down everything.

Don't pick only cheap options. Don't leave things out because you can't afford it or because you think you won't be able to afford it later. Pick the things you *want*, the things you *need,* and the things you *want in the future*. Note them down, and their costs.

For the larger purchases requiring a reserve, you can work out how long you want to wait until it's funded and how much money it would take each month to get there. Example: You want to take a vacation with your family. You shop and look around online and work out that it is going to cost you $7,000. You add on another $500 for random expenses while on vacation, so $7,500. You want to go at the end of summer, which is in 5 months. You already have $1,500 in a vacation fund leftover from an earlier vacation, so you only need $6,000 in 5 months. This works out to

$1,200 per month. This is now considered as an expense every month for the next 5 months.

The above makes for an interesting example that brings up a point: Monthly expenses do change! But they change on the basis of decided and desired spending and not as a reaction to a change in your level of income.

For emergency funds or reserves for potential, unplanned future needs, one idea is using a percentage of what remains after the expenses to live and the expenses to make money. Example: $3,000 in living expenses and $500 towards making more money on an income of $5,000 per month. That leaves $1,500. You decide on 7% to an emergency fund, so in this case it's $105 every month (7% of $1,500).

Now you take ALL of these monthly expenses from each of these steps or categories above and you add them up. This includes your debt repayment plans.

What is your total number here?

I think that's too low. It should be at least a little higher. Look over them again.

Remember, you are not setting this up based on what you "deserve" or seems "fair" or what's right according to your current or past level of income. You are also not spending money as reactions to bills due or debt repayments. You are consciously and intentionally planning to spend money on the desired and necessary expenses and funds to have the life you want to live - so don't skimp on it or cut yourself short. Look over all these expenses again and with that, I'll ask again.

What is your total number here?

Get your income up to this number and beyond. Don't increase your quality of life in ratio to your income, instead raise your income up to and past what is required for your desired quality of life.

IMPORTANT: Do not lower this number to make things easier for you. In fact, you should focus on finding more things to increase this number as time goes on.

"But my income isn't close to that number at all!!" you might shout. I understand. The number that most people will come up with is probably very close to what they are already spending anyway! The difference is that they are currently using debt to make these purchases, and there is no consideration for future income and income producing expenses.

With this new number you now need to focus all attention to one big and important goal: matching and then exceeding this number with your income. Do not give up, do not lessen the number. Do not forget everything and go back to the comfortable ignorance on the subject of your financial well-being. Don't continue being blindly led into a slow and uncertain financial future.

Add to your income and get it to that number and beyond.

CHAPTER 9: WHAT IS DEBT AND WHEN TO USE IT

The definition of DEBT: Something, almost always money, that is owed and needs to be repaid.

When to use it: Never if you can help it. Done, Next chapter!

Kidding.

Earlier, we touched on when to use debt: Using debt can make sense when there is an actual and definite return on the purchase, and the return was boosted by getting it now. For example if productivity and income could be increased by removing the time necessary to earn the funds needed, and the increased return was sufficient to justify not waiting to earn the amount needed first, borrowing could make sense. Where the increased value of getting it now was greater than the cost of taking on and then paying off the debt, then using debt can be a good option. Such a calculation should consider all the costs of the debt being taken on including fees, interest, collateral if used, etc.

There are many things that require more money than the average person has available when they decide to make the purchase.

Here are some examples of things that people often take on debt in order to buy:
- Home & home repairs
- Car
- College education

- Vacation
- Business expenses
- Starting a business
- Furniture
- Entertainment systems
- Loans to pay off or combine other loan payments
- Any many more

They all have one thing in common. They require more money than the typical person has readily available to whip out and pay in full.

Since the people offering a product want to make the sale, they sometimes have finance people or access to lines of credit that they can extend to help you use debt faster and easier in order to make the purchase. Many department stores and even online stores have their own credit cards.

I think we've talked enough earlier, in Chapter 5, on how bad an idea it is to use debt to finance lifestyle - so we won't dive into that again here.

Using debt could be a workable idea, but it depends on what is being financed.

The first thing to remember, is that when you use debt - you don't really, fully and actually own the thing you financed. Since you took a loan, you are required to continue to pay the lender back until it is considered paid off. For most people this translates into more hours worked and more time devoted for the sole purpose of making the money in order to pay off the debt. In almost every case the item is much more expensive when debt is used to purchase it. There are many cases where the purchaser ends up paying double, triple or more of the original cost.

You fully own something when you don't have to continue to work or pay for the right to keep it. In many cases it is part of the loan agreement that if you don't make the payments, the lender can take the thing that you used debt to purchase. In some cases, they can even take more than just the thing itself. When people fully face the truth of using debt to finance things, they see this grim reality. This is why we see such advice as "Avoid debt no matter what."

However, there is another truth: Fully avoiding debt can shut you off from some opportunities you might come across. For most people, fully avoiding debt at all cost, no matter what, might not even be possible. Debt exists! And the current economic system in the country in which you live is fully, 100% built on debt. At the time of this writing the United States is over $27,000,000,000,000 (27 Trillion) in debt.

Everyone around you uses debt, and debt is everywhere.

The wisdom comes into play when choosing your debt, and when to use it or avoid it.

Blanket statement: **Don't use debt to fund lifestyle.**

Lifestyle as defined in Chapter 1 is: The way someone lives their life and the things they spend money on to support their way of living. In the book I often say "fund lifestyle" and this means spending money on the things that allows someone to live the way they do, and often in a way that is more than just their needs.

If you are following the guidelines from Chapter 8, you will have funds and reserves set up to finance your bigger purchases down the road. But it can still happen that you come across something you need now and are unable to afford.

When you are convinced of the importance of a particular purchase, or come to terms with your need to buy something, and you don't have the money at that exact time, there are 3 options:
1. Use debt to get it now
2. Wait until you have the money later
3. Forget about it all together

We will skip option 3 as you don't need any instruction on how to do that - *just walk away*.

For the remaining options, how do you choose between the two?

First you find out what the actual cost of the debt will be. If it was financed, how much would it cost you in time, money, etc? Figure out the total cost as close as possible to what it would actually be, but without applying for the loan first. If you needed to apply and get a credit check and all that to get the actual terms of the loan, then get an estimated total cost. This total should include more than just the purchase price of the thing financed, but also the total amount of all the payments including interest and any other related fees. It should include loan origination fees or appraisal fees. Some loans might even come with a marketing fee. Know what they all are and how much total you will be paying for this purchase when all is said and done. There are online calculators and explanations you can use to find estimates. You can search online or look here: www.workingeconomics.com/resources-for-book-readers.

Next you determine your perceived value in this purchase. How valuable is it to you? This can be measured in potential returns later or some other way you find to measure it.

For example, some sort of personal enhancement such as job training, or learning new techniques in a technical field, could have tremendous returns down the road and could have a lot of value for you.

Another example could be in real estate. You would take a look for yourself at the potential value you would have in owning the property.

Now you compare these two values.

Don't just look at the cost in terms of monthly payments, but also the overall cost over the whole life of the loan. This is in terms of the commitment of payments as well as time required, and any other factors involved in the terms.

If you compare these values and see for yourself that it is a better decision financially to have it now, and that there is more to gain by making the purchase now instead of waiting to fund it with your income, then it can make sense to use debt to make this purchase.

There is one more important aspect of debts to close this chapter: Where debts can be avoided, it is almost always a better decision not to add the debt. Where possible, it is better to fund it yourself through your own income sources.

Following the principles in the earlier chapters might have a little bit longer runway to getting and keeping the things you want, as opposed to using debt to acquire them. But, by doing so you fully own and control the things you get. Further, if you use and keep using the principles from earlier, you will have the funds and continue to have the reserves to actually purchase the things you need.

I do know there are many rich people and businessmen that have used and hold massive debts. They use these debts to fund their businesses, lifestyle, and massive net worth. But I believe that these riches are built off of a faulty system. Even the untouchable wealthy, with over leveraged debts, are still the effect of whoever issued their debts when they come to collect, or request favors.

In summary, where it makes sense to use the debt as covered, don't fear it. Where possible, patience and earning the money first will most likely be the better option.

CHAPTER 10: METHODS OF HANDLING DEBT

The first part of handling debt is having an understanding and your own workout of how you are going to be spending your money - you will need to have finished Chapter 8 for that. Go back now if you need to.

You do not give up necessities to pay off debt. Repaying debt is far less important than staying alive. You can however remove or reduce lifestyle purchases and other extra purchases to pay more on your debts as you want.

There are two major points made concerning handling debts in this book: 1) Make the plan to handle a debt before you incur it and 2) Have a way to handle your existing debts and stick to it.

We will now take up how to handle existing debts.

The wrong ways to handle debts:

Pretending debts don't exist while continuing to add to them. I am referring to the use of credit to finance purchases and lifestyle. This is the person who continues to charge on credit after it has already become clear to someone else looking at the picture, that there is no hope of paying off what is already owed.

Maybe this person considers they are unable to live without continuing to use credit due to some emergency, setback, or lack of income. Maybe the person is oblivious or miseducated. Maybe the person got a little carried away and now has a balance larger than they ever thought they could handle and so sort of surrenders. Maybe this person plans to just rack it all up and then walk away. Whatever the reason or motivation, they create an ever-increasing amount of debt.

The person might be making minimum payments, but more than likely this person either has an auto-pay set up so they can forget about it, is not making payments, or is making less than the minimum payments "when they can."

Average payments in the average way. This is the most common way I have seen people try to handle their debts. They either A) Make the minimum payments shortly before they are due or B) Pay a set number that is the minimums plus a little extra to try to pay it off faster. Something like $300 a month which is $100 for the minimum plus an extra $200 because that's the extra money they can afford.

This isn't based on any plan with an end goal or date for getting the debts killed off. They just keep throwing as much money at the debt as they feel they can afford. I have a friend who, at one point, had five lines of credit and was paying a little above the minimum payments on each card every month. This was a smart person but unfortunately, he did not see the mistake of paying a little extra on each card. After a little talking it over, he saw how by paying just a little extra on each card - he prolonged the life of each card's debt. That he would continue having all five debts until they were all paid off and would be paying interest on each one the whole time. With a little persuasion, he started putting his extra resources into one card at a time and was then murdering that particular debt and its interest quicker.

Paying just the minimums, or the minimums plus a little extra, is what the banks are expecting *and prefer*. The problem with this is that you are going according to their plan. And in their plan, they are trying to get you to pay them back as slowly as possible and over the longest period of time.

The banks (and remember credit card companies ARE banks) would much prefer that you pay them as little as possible each month - because in the long run they will make much more money that way.

The banks *do not* want you to pay off the debt.

You know that little notification on the credit card bill that tells you: if you only pay the minimums it will take you 36 months or however long, and you will pay however many more thousands extra in interest? They don't put that there to encourage you to pay faster. They don't put that there because they don't want you to get ripped off or because they feel guilty. They're on the bills because it's the law.

They are required by law to notify you of the effects of only paying the minimums. It comes from the Credit Card Accountability Responsibility and Disclosure Act of 2009 - look it up if you want.

Crazy mode - throwing nearly all money at debt. You might have done it this way or seen this done. As an example, someone starves themselves and gives up lots to throw as much money as they can at their debts. They don't go out with friends after work - they stay home instead. They don't eat out, they don't spend any money on fun. They give up everything so they can scrape as much money together as possible and dump it all on the debt every month.

This is admirable but can put someone in unnecessary risk.

By not spending money as we outlined in Chapter 8 and using all of their money toward credit card debt, they have no money. Not having money is a recipe for adding on more debt.

What happens to this person who is throwing all of their money every month onto credit card debt when a needed or unexpected expense shows up - something they can't or don't want to put off? Something they need to pay for. What happens? They charge it on credit!

They charge it because it was the only option. They justify the increased debt since they had made that extra credit available and so they can now use it. They either open a new credit card, or use an existing card with credit now available from paying down its balance. This is looking at credit as the same as cash, or at least similar to it - which it is not. On average, credit is 22% more expensive than cash - per year (If that's confusing, that is how much most people are paying on their credit cards in interest - 22% of the debt per year.)

This method normally gets put into play when someone "wakes up" to the amount of debt they have, feels uncomfortable about it, and swears to go all in to slay the beast as fast as possible. They decide that getting rid of the debt in the next 8 months instead of 12 months is worth self-sacrifice.

Yes, debt is expensive, but why go about handling it in a way that opens you up to potential pitfalls in the future or risks to your wellbeing in addition to your money?

Not having a plan for spending and using your income, and just spending money towards debt in ratio to how much money you have sets you up to be an effect of uncertainties in the future. Having and following a plan is the way to go, and part of that plan should include not spending all of your money on debt as fast as you can.

Some workable ways for handling debt:

First and foremost, is getting your spending squared away. Chapter 8 (How to spend money - What things you should spend your money on) is the second most important chapter in this book, after the Chapter on the Laws of course. If you haven't worked out your spending yet, then you really should go back and do it.

The second thing is getting busier, doing more work, producing more, marketing more, selling more, working harder. All of this in the direction of making more money. After getting your "how you spend" straightened away, your focus should be on how to increase your income and now. Don't even wait a week - find ways to get in more money and get it now. If you feel stuck, you should have another look at the Laws and maybe you'll get some ideas for areas to improve or things you can do.

Next is how you spend your money on the debt itself. This was not described in the spending chapter since it is gone over here, in a moment.

If you are set on eliminating debt as fast as possible then you should have the highest possible amount from your spending workout devoted to paying off debt. I do of course recommend still having some sort of regular addition to reserves, no matter what.

It is worthwhile to see if you can get your debt to be as cheap as possible - meaning the lowest interest rates. It is much faster and easier to pay off a loan when you are paying 3%, or even 0% interest, versus paying 22%.

I use credit cards in most of the examples since this is the most common debt people have that they are trying to get rid of. But if there were other types of debt someone wanted to eliminate quickly these methods would work on those just as well.

There are mainly three methods I have heard of proving workable for others:

Pay just the minimums since the loan finances something that produces more income than the cost of the debt: This applies to things such as commercial real estate or low interest business loans. If you are already in a scenario where you have income producing real estate that was financed with a loan - it will probably make more sense to pay the minimums than paying it off. There is also the potential that interest payments on certain loans could be tax write-offs.

Example: If the mortgage on the property is $600,000 and the interest rate is 4% - this will be a monthly payment of about $2,800. It is a three-unit property, generating $1,500 in income from each unit - so it makes $4,500 a month. Using the income to pay for the loan leaves you with $1,700 per month for expenses, repairs, fees, and any profit. In this case, it might make sense not to pay more than the regular monthly payment.

Example: There's a small business and before the owner read this book, she took out a loan of $100,000. She already put that money into the business. The terms are 60 months at 5% interest per year. This makes the monthly payments nearly $1,900 per month. The total interest paid in the end is about $13,000 (after 5 years). This small business makes $215,000 per year, or $18,000 per month. This business owner sees that if she doesn't aggressively pay off the debt, and instead uses some money from the income to pay for an additional employee, she doesn't have to be in the office. She is then able to separate herself from the day-to-day and go do other things. In this case it makes more sense to use part of the $18,000 per month on the business itself rather than towards getting rid of the debt faster.

Pay off the smallest balances first method: Let's say you have 5 credit cards. The balances are $500, $2,000, $2,500, $4,000, and $10,000. With this method you would be paying the minimums on each credit card, and then taking the rest of the money you devoted to paying off debt this month and applying it to the lowest card - in this case the card with the $500 balance.

After the $500 card was paid in full, leaving a zero balance, you would take all the money which was being paid monthly to the $500 card and apply it to the $2,000 card. This is while still making the minimum payments on the other cards.

It's important that when a card gets paid off, you don't lessen the amount you are devoting to paying off debts the following month. It might be easy to think that since you no longer need to pay towards the $500 card after it got paid off, you now have that extra monthly money for other things. I hope you don't think that way at this point of the book, if you even did before.

Once the $2,000 card is paid off, you continue to make the minimum payments on the other remaining cards and you apply all additional funds (the minimum payment amounts from card 1 and 2 plus any additional payment you were making) to the next card - the $2,500 balance one.

Continue like this all the way until they are all gone.

With this method you are doing the smallest balance first and working up towards the highest balance at the end with the idea that the removal of each payment for each card along the way gives you more comfort and requires less attention.

If it's credit cards you are handling this way, I would advise not to close the card when the debt is gone. Leave it open, just don't use it. Toss it in that new dedicated shoe box for "credit cards I have paid off but didn't close and am not using." As stated earlier in the book, credit cards don't bite. Leaving them open doesn't mean that you will wake up one day at 2:30am to find yourself hunched over your computer making purchases in your sleep and racking up the debt again.

Closing a card does have an impact on your credit score, if this is important to you, or if you play the credit score game.

If you are leaving the card open, then you should remember that most banks require you to make a purchase on it before a year passes - or they might close the card on their own. For this reason, you don't cut it up and toss it out. In nearly a year you will need to go buy a coffee with it, pay off the balance, and put the card back in the shoe box.

Paying off the highest interest first method: This is similar to the last one, but instead of focusing on the lowest balance, you focus on the highest interest rate.

You do the same thing with paying the minimums each month on all, but you pool the rest of the money devoted to paying off debt that month to the card with the highest interest rate. Once that one is gone you then take up the next highest interest rate and so on, much like the previous method, but focusing on highest interest rates instead of lowest balances.

There is a fourth method, my method. It is by far my preferred approach. It however requires considerably more discipline. Without discipline it won't work at all. However, with discipline this way provides the most security and comfort out of all the methods I know of paying off debt.

The big-baller, shot-caller method: This is how I have handled personal debts, so it gets the coolest name.

In a nutshell: collect a large savings in a reserve, while the existing debts are moved to low, or no interest. Getting 0% or low interest might be more straightforward with credit cards, but it works with other types of loans too.

Many banks offer a 0% interest rate on introductory offers for a year, and some offer more than a year. To get these you do need to qualify, meaning a decent enough credit score to get approved. Some banks offer 1% or 3% loans to "consolidate." Consolidate just means combining. It's using a larger loan to pay off multiple smaller loans. Consolidating with a loan can work as well as low interest credit cards. You might need to shop around a bit as the goal is to get all of the credit cards or debts covered by 0% or at least a very low interest rate.

After getting the 0% or low interest card/loan set up and your debt moved over, you'll now be faced with the first test of your discipline: Not adding more debt. If you were experiencing stress before due to the large monthly payments, and they were on high interest cards - you will suddenly see a massive shift in your finances as the required monthly payments come way, way down. You need to ensure you don't use any remaining credit lines or your freed-up cash to purchase things. You need to make sure that you don't spend your cash on other things since the stress from the debt has lessened and there is less demand on your finances for the moment.

The stress may have been relieved, but after a year it will come back (when the lower interest rate expires). This method is about getting rid of the expensive debt, not shifting it around on low interest offers endlessly.

You make the minimum payments on each of the loans or lines of credit, and not any more. You take all available cash and resources and money and put it into a special account specifically reserved for paying off this debt.

The purpose of this is simple: if the shit hits the fan - you have cash. Earlier I said that when someone uses all of their cash to pay a credit card, they could fall victim to charging it back up when they come across an unexpected expense. By stashing the money in an account instead, you have cash available. If there is a sudden emergency or a need to finance a big, unexpected purchase you have the cash available to do so instead of needing to take on more credit card debt for it.

This is the second test of your discipline: continuing to add to this reserve and not spending it. Before too long, you will have a large bank account balance. You might be tempted to buy that thing you have had your eye on or take that vacation. If you want to do those things, I can't stop you - I don't even know where you live. But remember: don't finance lifestyle with this new cash surplus, and any money you use for fun now will need to be replaced from your income later.

By the time the 0% offer is getting close to expiring you should have a nice little pile of cash saved up. If it is enough to pay off your debt in one go, then go for it. Make sure you don't zero out your bank account to do so, so you can still eat and have money for the other things you are supposed to be allocating for. It's better to pay the interest a little longer and still have some money, than to dump all accounts everywhere to avoid one month of interest.

If there isn't enough to clean off the debt, then you pay off what you can and repeat. You go at it for another year - same method. Your credit score will be looking better with the massive chunk you just paid off and you will be able to get approved for some other sort of loan or intro offer. You might even be able to just call the bank and get them to extend your current offer or get a better one.

This method doesn't work without a good interest rate. If you can't get a good interest rate, you will have to use one of the other two methods - lowest balance first, or highest interest first. And in all cases, it is important to keep up your other allocations and some sort of reserves as per the chapter on how to spend money. I keep making this point because it is important.

One more point of note on this: often when a credit card, and sometimes another type of loan, is paid off there is still an interest payment required for one more month. Make sure that when you pay off the last month you keep attention on it until the next month's statement comes and shows you that you owe nothing.

Advices/Opinions on paying common types of larger debts:

There are certain things people have large debts for as they are normal, expected, and part of how our society runs. While I recommend avoiding the below debts in most circumstances where possible, here are my opinions on how to handle them.

These get their own little section as they are special kinds of debts. These types of debts are also large and carried by most people.

Home loan: Ensure you aren't paying more than you can afford based on your allocations and your workout from the chapter on spending. After that just pay it as a necessity, it comes out of your income as part of the first allocations. I wouldn't pay extra, and I wouldn't pay less or be behind - just pay it regularly and monthly. It's also a good idea to consider the interest rate on your home mortgage. If it is very high perhaps you should refinance to a lower rate.

Car loan: Very much the same as the home loan, with a small extra: I would recommend a reserve for the paying off the car loan faster. Applying the principle of the *big baller, shot caller method* of handling debts. This is a monthly payment that needs to be made, until it doesn't anymore. A car is a much easier thing to pay off then a house and is a monthly payment that can be eliminated in a reasonably short period of time.

Student loan: This one unfortunately depends largely on the terms of the loan as well as who issued it. More unfortunately still, most student loan debt is set up in such a way that they are very difficult to pay off quickly. Sometimes, but not often enough, the person with the student loan successfully graduates and gets a career where they can use their degree. Maybe they make decent money as a result and they don't have much concern for the student loan. Because student loan debts are so variable, I can't offer much in terms of what would work best for you. But, here is something: For the most part, pay the minimum payment and treat it as an uncomfortable, aching annoyance that you just have to deal with. Stick to the terms and eventually it will go away, or maybe you will die before then (dark humor.) Do not sacrifice other allocations or reserves to pay this loan or to pay it faster. A lot of student loans are quite forgiving if you miss a month here or there. Some people treat this with such importance that they can never miss a payment and feel they must pay extra. To them I say: relax on this one a little.

Loans from friends or family: Follow the terms as agreed upon - don't waiver as there is a personal relationship tied to this one. Messing it up can cost more than just a moment of upset. Start a reserve to add extra money to, in order to pay this off faster - given that the agreement allows for that.

Payday loans: Don't ever get one, ever. These are the scummiest, saddest, and most harmful loans out there. They charge massive interest, and the loan comes due in a very short period of time. If you find yourself feeling like you need to get a payday loan - don't. Short of selling your body or doing illegal things - most options to come up with money to handle whatever is stressing you right now, are better alternatives than a payday loan. If for some reason you already have a payday loan, then you need to get out of it quickly and stay out. You can borrow money from friends, family, boss, co-workers, or you can do things to make money now to cover it. Sell things, work extra - even more than you already are, etc.

Some sort of court ordered payment plan for something legally binding: If you are found by the court to owe somebody and some sort of payment plan is worked out - or if you messed up on taxes and owe the IRS a bill then do this: pay it by the terms exactly as they are written and agreed. No more and no less. Pay the monthly at the beginning of the month, not right before it is due. Pay it through trackable and verifiable means, such as bank transfers - never cash. And continue on until the agreement is fulfilled. Meanwhile, focus on making more money.

I hope these help.

When you consider using debt in the future, I urge you to think with these methods. Ask yourself how you will handle this debt, what is the true and total cost of the debt, and work out a plan of action before you swipe that credit card or sign that loan agreement.

Most importantly, you need to increase your income - you need to add more money coming in on a regular basis. That will help you remove existing debt, and also remove the need for debt in the future.

CHAPTER 11: INCREASING INCOME

The three most common things I hear from people on the subject of finance are: "how do I handle my debt?" "how do I make more money?" and "how do I invest and what should I invest in?" We've gone over debt and so we are now going to go over increasing income. In the chapter after this one we will talk about investing.

INCOME is: Money received, especially when on a regular basis or schedule.

I want you to know it is totally possible to increase your income.

You need to know that there is so much money out there in the world. There is so much money in the United States that gets spent every day.

On the 4th of July, a single day, over $1 Billion of beer gets drunk (a lot of people get drunk too). For the rest of the year there is $20 Billion spent at bars, and $1.9 Billion at nightclubs.

In 1 year within the United States there is: $26 Billion spent on birdwatching, $3 Billion for bags of ice, $62 Billion on cosmetics like makeup, $2 Billion on chewing gum, $80.5 Billion on the lottery, $31 Billion goes to buying flowers, $2.4 Billion to buying hotdogs from the store, and much more.

This is billions, as in $1,000,000,000.

There is no shortage of money.

The problem is in looking at individual spenders only and not at markets. An individual might not spend that much money on playing fantasy football in a year, but collectively the people who play fantasy football spend $4.6 Billion dollars on it. There is another chapter later on the subject of markets that goes into more detail on this. The point here is that there is money. Lots of it!

Now, a definition of success is accomplishing a purpose. But there is another definition: the attainment of wealth.

Economic Law #12: *Your success in business is based on your ability to find, create or strengthen a demand, having goods or services to meet the demand and getting them marketed, sold and delivered in volume and with high quality.*

The unfortunate truth with this is: if you rely solely on the income produced by working directly for an employer, then your income is most likely limited. Your income is limited for two reasons:

1. Your income is directly tied to your available time to work for the employer as well as the employer's willingness to keep you employed and keep paying you. There is only so much work time available in a week.
2. You can only increase that particular income stream by increasing the perceived value of your labor, service, etc. in the eyes of the person who cuts the paychecks and increasing his or her demand for what you offer.

Some people try to increase this type of income by working more hours. Some do it by trying to get more education, or a college degree they feel they were missing. Some people try to do such a good job and get noticed that they get a promotion and with it an increased paycheck - but sometimes the hard work doesn't get noticed.

Per Economic Law #27: *Anywhere there is an exchange of money for goods or services these Laws apply.* Income from an employer is a transfer of money - the Economic Laws apply. That means it is possible to take charge and increase that source of income.

Why is the employer paying for the work? What demand is being met? Can the employer's demand be strengthened? (The answer to strengthening a demand is in Economic Law #5: *The perceived increase in ability to live or quality of life by the purchaser).* If a demand is strengthened, can the employee deliver enough to meet that demand? If so he or she is halfway there.

The employee, in order to fully take charge of his or her own income, must also market (make known the existence of) these facts as described above to the employer. The employee must also sell (as in explain why it is worthwhile and guide to the decision) the employer on the raise or promotion.

Not doing these things is leaving it up to chance, or hoping that the too busy, overworked, and distracted employer will happen to notice the hard work being done.

However, if someone was to work hard and get their income increased by their employer and that was the only way they counted on to increase income - they are still limited. They are still affected by the 2 points above, time availability and perceived value to the employer.

To remove the cap, or limit on the income, it is necessary to include an additional source. Everyone is capable of finding, creating, or strengthening demands in a market and then supplying goods or services to meet these demands. That activity is all a business really is - and since anyone can do it, you can too. If you don't have a business, product, "side hustle," or whatever you want to call it, you should get one started.

The average American spends 35 hours per week watching TV. This is more than enough time to allow for some creating and strengthening of another source of income, or business. Just about everyone can create and build a business even while working another job full-time during the week. The difference between doing it or not is in seeing the value of doing it and having the personal need for it. It is easy to get distracted by other things. It is much harder to use this valuable "free time" on things other than relaxing or having fun.

Why is "free time" in quotes? Because free time is actually paid-for-time. People buy their free time using the money they earned from their time on the job. People with more needs than they can support in a regular 40-hour work week end up with less "free time" - they require more work and time to pay for their ability to live. They have less money and less paid-for-time.

The vast majority of people choose to spend all of this paid-for-time purchasing and consuming products or services that give other people money, not them.

It is important to relax and have fun, but there are too many opportunities wasted by not using at least some of the available paid-for-time to build and strengthen more sources of income.

You know people, or can at least find them, who have a demand for things that you can offer or supply and make money in return. Those people know more people they can connect you with who also need goods or services that you can supply.

There are needs out there. So much money gets spent every day. It is very possible, using some of your available paid-for-time, to tap into the massive amounts of money being exchanged daily in the markets throughout the country and the world.

I strongly urge you at this point, with a hopefully different perspective than at the beginning of this book, to place a bookmark right here and go back to Chapter 3. Re-read the Economic Laws and see how many ideas and different possible activities you can come up with. See how many different ways you can think of to apply these Laws and use them to make money. Find which ones were missed in earlier attempts and caused difficulties or points of failure. Or, identify how others have failed in making money by being unaware of these Laws.

Go ahead and put your bookmark here.

Do you have some ideas? Did you think of some ways you can use these to make more money? How about any points that were missed in the past that might have caused difficulties or failures?

To help illustrate this further I will lay out an example of starting up a new business, product, or source of income. The following is not a formula, or the magic steps to take - it is just an example of using the Economic Laws to start making additional income.

For this example, we will talk about a woman named Sophia.

Sophia has a nice job with decent pay. She is the office manager for a large construction company and oversees several administrative employees. The main service of the company is repairing and upgrading hotels. She has been examining her expenses as well as the things she would like to fund in the future and sees that she needs to make more money than she is now.

She has started a reserve fund to pay for future ways of increasing income and is on the lookout for opportunities.

She is familiar with the industry her company is in and is herself quite interested in it. She is friends with a lot of the employees as well as the boss and has learned a lot over her years of working there. One thing that she learned is that hotels always have art hanging on the walls in the rooms and hallways. This is something that most think is unimportant. She remembers hearing about a time the company did a massive upgrade of a hotel and the hotel was planning to replace all of the art in the process. She remembers this because someone had told her that they got to take some of the old paintings home since they were all being thrown away.

She looks into this further.

Sophia finds that most hotels the company does business with upgrade their art when they upgrade their buildings. They do this to modernize and not feel stale or outdated. She finds that getting the new art has actually been a problem for the managers and owners of these hotels. Finding and then hanging inexpensive paintings on the walls is not something hotel owners want to be distracted by when they are going through such a large project.

She has a bright idea. She can supply the art. She can provide a service of planning the art and decorations, getting the art, and getting it placed throughout the hotel.

She has a good relationship with her boss at the company and gets his willingness to connect her with the hotel manager of a current construction project.

She isn't an artist herself, but always felt that she had an artistic eye. She shops around online and finds some suppliers of paintings at wholesale prices.

She meets the hotel manager and arrives with a portfolio she put together to showcase different art styles and options. The hotel manager is impressed that Sophia took the time to find different pieces that complemented the new upgrades being done by the construction company. The hotel manager is pleased as the options presented just make sense and a lot of his time has been saved by not having to do this personally. Sophia also did the math on what was needed for the entire project. 10 rooms with 2 paintings per room, and 5 paintings in the hallways on each floor. There are 10 floors and so 250 paintings are needed, plus an additional 5 for the lobby, so 255 total. She gives the quote for 255 paintings at $33,500 - which includes hanging the art.

The hotel manager does some math and sees how good of a deal it is and accepts Sophia's proposal.

She gets a down payment and is off to get it delivered. She buys the art which costs her $80 a piece on average ($20,400). She buys this art using the down payment and some of the money she has been saving to fund income producing activities or products.

She grabs one of her friends and her cousin to come help hang the art, which is done after regular work hours. She shows them how she wants it done and how to do it. She pays them each $100 a night and the three of them working together complete hanging all the art after 8 days. Her friend and cousin got extra money for working an extra hour or so each night and are happy. Sophia paid them $800 each, so $1600 total.

She meets up with the hotel manager and collects the rest of the payment due. She made a profit of $11,500.

She is very happy. The hotel manager is happy. Her friend and cousin are happy.

She takes this money and uses it as per Chapter 8 on how to spend money. She replenishes her Opportunity Fund. She buys something nice to acknowledge and thank her boss for setting up the meeting with the hotel manager.

She creates a system and eventually this becomes a normal activity. Down the road her art projects are almost being sold directly by the construction company when they are doing their initial service offering.

Now this story leaves out the blood, sweat, and tears - of which Sophia did endure, but she has a successful business of her own. She didn't quit her other job until it made financial sense to devote all of her time to her art business. She kept on very good terms with the boss from the construction company and still gets many leads from them, but the business she created has its own marketing and sales and so she finds most of her own work.

She applied Economic Law #12, whether she knew the principles in this book existed or not (but in this case she did, so it made it easier).

She identified a demand, got a product that met the demand and got it marketed using the construction company. She sold it to the hotel managers, she delivered a high-quality service, and then figured out how to increase her volume of sales by adding her own sales and marketing efforts.

Many other examples and stories like this exist. Someone does not need to have a friendly boss who is willing to help out in order to start up another source of income.

Someone could find that half of the fences in his neighborhood are needing paint and go to his neighbors on the weekends and offer his service to paint the fences. Over time he finds fences needing repairs and offers that service too. After a while he is known as the fence-guy and has a successful business going.

Another: Someone is a really good cook and has a home-made barbecue sauce that anyone who has ever tried it swears it's the best in the world. After a while he decides to pursue selling it as his business. He finds where people go to try and buy new foods: festivals, art shows, food trucks, farmer's markets, etc. He works out how to make large batches and starts selling and marketing his product. He makes an online store for people to reorder from, and he includes his website on the packaging of the bottles. Over time the amount of consistent sales increases more and more and more.

Another: Someone learned there is a huge market for buying rugs. He finds a supply of rugs that he can get for wholesale prices, and by trial and error and asking around finds places where he can go to display his rugs out of his truck and make sales. He does this on the weekends and some evenings in addition to his day job. He makes a surprising amount of extra money doing so. Eventually he finds he can make more money doing this than his other job and so puts more time into selling rugs and travels with a trailer carrying his supply to expand his market reach.

Another: A young man goes door to door to sell lawn care on weekends.

Another: Learning website services and delivering these to people who need websites.

The examples go on endlessly. There is so much money getting spent every day and so many people have so many demands.

People often have trouble "coming up with business ideas" when they are trying to figure out how to market themselves or their particular skills. Instead, why not focus on finding, creating, or strengthening a demand. If someone finds a demand, they can then figure out how they can supply it or if they even want to. You would probably have a better time coming up with an idea to supply an existing demand, versus trying to come up with an idea without also seeing if there is a demand or market for it.

Now what if someone already is self-employed, or has their own business, product, "side hustle," or whatever you want to call it?

Then it is a matter of increasing the income from that source. It's likely that putting money into this business can help speed up and increase income from it. But the money that's going into it should directly contribute to increasing the marketing, sales, customer awareness, volume of delivery, quality of product, or word of mouth.

Dumping money into increasing a supply without marketing leaves someone with more products to sell, but not more sales - this can be costly.

I asked you earlier to put in a bookmark and look at the Laws. Did you do that for your own business and see what points can be applied or increased to add more income from this source? Your answer to more income is somewhere in Chapter 3.

If you feel stuck or confused, you can always contact me through social media (@AuthorJeremyPS) or at: www.workingeconomics.com/contact.

CHAPTER 12: INVESTING - ADDING SOURCES OF INCOME

From Chapter 1, INVEST: Putting money into something with the hopes of getting a profit as a result. Investments are the things that you put the money into to try to get a profit.

The first investment is your own business - as per the previous chapter on increasing income.

If you don't have a business, get one going. That is the best thing you can invest in.

Owning a business will just about ALWAYS, outperform stocks, bonds, speculative real estate purchases, REITS, mutual funds, CDs, savings accounts, life insurance, cryptocurrencies, currency trading, precious metals, etc.

All of those other types of investments are things that are out of your control. A business you own is in your control. You cannot directly determine or affect the outcome of how a mutual fund will perform. You can directly control how a business performs and increase its production and income.

People fail to see owning a business is an investment for a few reasons:
1. They look at owning a business as another job instead of an income producing asset.
2. They are fully sold on the *neeeed* to put money into stocks, or other traditional investment instruments which are actually built on making money for the banker or financial advisor.

3. They already own a business and just think of it as their main source of income.

Paint this on the wall or tattoo it on the inside of your eyelids:

YOUR FIRST INVESTMENT SHOULD BE YOUR OWN BUSINESS

YOUR MOST VALUABLE INVESTMENT IS A BUSINESS YOU OWN

Let's look at some basic math for this:

Let's say you have a business that only makes you $30,000 in profit per year. Some would consider this a low amount.

To make that kind of return on the stock market would require something like $428,000 invested with a 7% annual return. But it isn't that straightforward. If it's in a managed fund you pay a fee, probably in the neighborhood of 1%. So, the $30,000 minus the 1% fee comes down to $25,720. You then also need to sell enough stocks to convert that gain into cash. Luckily the fee to make the trades isn't much, but it does cost you something.

Then after it's turned into cash and you take it out you now have to pay capital gains tax. Let's say you pay 15% of the gain, leaving you now with $21,862.

I wouldn't put that much importance on the taxes in this example since taxes are part of living in the world and should be planned for and addressed head on, not forgotten about or by wishing they'd go away. Taxes would also be required in a business, however there is an important benefit to keep in mind. There are a large number of tax deductions available to a small business which can reduce your tax burden significantly. Please see a tax professional for further information on the tax benefits of owning your own business. But it's possible that the tax deductions available to a small business owner could eliminate a large amount of required taxes on that $30,000 income.

Now there are other things about this $428,000 investment into stocks. What are the odds of there being a dip and that value getting shredded? The likelihood of there being a big dip in the next 3 years is very high - almost a sure thing. Can you keep your cool when you see the value of your $428,000 suddenly turn into $376,640 over the span of 3 months? That is exactly what happened to the money in the Dow Jones Industrial Average (A very popular investment fund that serves as an indicator of the overall stock market) in January through March of 2018. It happened again in 2019, where a sum of $428,000 would be turned into $359,520. Not to mention the 2020 crash where the $428,000 would've been turned into $279,136 in just one month. At times like these it can be hard to take out $30,000 for the year, as that would require selling your shares at painfully reduced prices. You would probably decide not to sell and instead feel the need to keep it invested, hoping to make up the loss over the coming months or years.

Also, if you are taking money out then you are losing out on compound interest - most money experts recommend leaving your money invested.

If you listen to your favorite billionaire investor you would learn that his winning way is to throw money into a stock and forget about it - keep it invested for the long haul. You will also learn that you need a large amount of money to really make investing in stocks worthwhile.

You might be thinking, *"Gosh, this guy really hates stocks - he must have been burned."* On the contrary. I messed around with it some time back and luckily ended up with positive returns. The main thing I learned was that casinos were much more fun and required much less time and stress - they didn't consume my thoughts the way stocks did. I saw how fast money could be lost on risky picks, and also how fast money could be gained on lucky choices. Overall, I got out ahead, but it was all speculative (involving risk and guessing rather than based on knowledge or productivity.)

I am not recommending casinos, or gambling, I am just trying to make a point.

Stock advisors and news publications exist to convince you that some expert has somehow figured out the formula for predicting stock trends and what the next successful big winner is going to be. You might have seen an ad somewhere on the internet making you feel guilty or foolish if you decide to miss out on the next big stock picks from experts. These experts share their top 5 greatest predictions with zillions of percent in returns. You see five big wins that span a period of decades, but they never show their hundreds of losers.

There is another aspect that makes stocks and traditional investments so appealing: you don't have to do anything after you send them your money. I'm sure a lot of people would much rather send their money off, kick back and relax, and not have to do more work on their own sources of income. I admit that I would much prefer that myself. If the returns were true or guaranteed, then I would. The problem is they're not, and that is the reason I am so insistent on owning investments directly.

Back to businesses.

I've never heard of a small business owner having a year in which not only did she make $0 in income but also lost $70,000 of her assets because the market performed unfavorably. If you lose at business, you just don't make any money - you don't also now lose your assets. Some might choose to leverage assets or dip into savings to try to save a business or some such. But they don't get their money or savings ripped away on the simple basis of being unsuccessful or other factors out of their control - which is the case with stocks.

Ideally you can get a business going in which your personal involvement in the day to day operations is not required, while still making income from it. The amount of money your business provides you might not be the sexy figures promised by stockbrokers, but it can be consistent and much, much, much more certain in addition to being under your control.

Another big perk is you can set up a business making $30,000 or more a year without having put at risk $428,000 of your savings or assets to do so.

Yet another big perk is the ability to make purchases which are business expenses and can lessen your taxes. The purpose of this book is not tax advice, so you will need to hit the *search engine of choice* and research that on your own.

Again:

YOUR FIRST INVESTMENT SHOULD BE YOUR OWN BUSINESS

YOUR MOST VALUABLE INVESTMENT IS A BUSINESS YOU OWN

Now, what about other things besides a business? More businesses! But let's also look at a few other popular investment choices.

Real Estate: When it comes to real estate, I am in favor of properties that produce income on a regular schedule, but not on properties where the purchase is made on the hope that it will go up in value to be sold later for a profit. I would lean in the direction of buying properties to hold onto forever and continuing to make income from them indefinitely. Now, when owning an income producing property, there are times when selling the property can give you a significant profit since the value has increased over time. If you were to sell such a property in order to generate the money to purchase a bigger and better property, this could be a good idea. Another thing to remember on this is that when your property has gone up in value because of the market, other purchase options will likely cost more as well.

Precious Metals (gold, silver, etc.): Every now and again people become crazed about putting money into precious metals. This is usually due to a fear that the currency or government might collapse or lose value. People believe that there will still be value in gold, silver, etc. There is some truth in this. Your grandparents paid cents at the gas pump and we pay dollars. In the 1950's the dollar had about 10 times more spending power than it does now. The cost of gold and silver has consistently gone up over time. The problem with precious metals is they don't generate income and the returns are still speculative, and over a long time.

Stocks: The thing that makes stocks, and other publicly traded items, so attractive is that it doesn't require work from the person. You put your money in and forget about it (or try to forget about it). So many people are fixed on using stocks

- so if someone was insistent on having an involvement in the stock market, I can see two potentially workable ways:

1. Amassing a savings while waiting for a dip or low point in the market and then investing and forgetting about it for most of the rest of your life
2. Buying dividend yielding stocks. In this case the owner of the stock receives a little bit of money each quarter for owning it. You have to put a lot of money into this to make it worthwhile - a lot meaning a million plus. The stocks bought would come with cash dividends paid quarterly. You would need to do the math to see how long you would need to hold the stock to make it worthwhile, but as a minimum you can treat it as a place to hold your money that pays you. There is a risk that the value of the stock goes down and along with it the value of your initial investment. Example: Microsoft currently pays dividends of about $0.55 a share. A share costs about $200. To make $30,000 a year from this you would need 13,636 shares which costs about $2,727,000.

Art: Investing in art is for the extremely wealthy who have so much money they need places to hide it, ways to avoid taxes, or they invest in speculative returns.

Currency trading (including cryptocurrencies like bitcoin): Some people buy large quantities of currency in developing countries and economies on the hope that later down the road the value will go up. This is much like investing in gold and other precious metals. It is not the same thing as owning precious metals, but it's very similar in that no actual income is produced by it, and it is speculative in nature. Cryptocurrencies like bitcoin were all the rage not too long ago and some made millions of dollars - but similar to other speculative trades, the ones that made millions got their wealth at the cost of other people losing theirs. The marketplace for cryptocurrencies is very fast, and values can change by huge amounts in very short periods of time. It's open and trading 24/7, which means you can wake up one morning to find a sudden increase in wealth or having lost it all. Currency trading is a risk and a gamble. It does not produce income, and any gains or losses are actually transfers of wealth.

Angel Investing: This is funding companies just getting started, it is called angel investing. This is acting as a private investor for someone starting a company. It is buying parts of a privately owned company and not publicly traded stocks as in the stock market. Normally people who invest in new companies have a lot of money to invest with and make risky bets. According to Forbes magazine, only 5-10 percent of angel investments are profitable - meaning more than 90% of them result in a loss - very risky. However, since angel investing is privately done between people, an investor would be able to meet the new business owner or owners face to face, learn who they are, and make assessments on the company. I believe the success rate could be improved. I believe the high failure rate mentioned is due to risky gambles on companies with no aims to produce income. I would shy away from tech start-ups and companies created on the basis of getting big and being sold quickly. I can see getting behind providing necessary funding for someone to get a goods-or-service oriented business geared towards making profit and aligned with the Economic Laws. As an investor I would look to see how aligned the company would be with the Laws. I would get an ownership stake in the company and get the profits shared. I can see being personally involved and turning this opportunity more into a business partner or becoming a part owner instead of just investing and sitting back. I would want to make sure it worked and made a profit. There are thousands and thousands of tech related start-ups, with most of them failing, so I would stay out of that arena. I would be more in favor of a product related company that can sell goods or services near or at the beginning.

Providing loans: Acting as a bank and lending someone your money can be risky. Often this happens when someone is unable to get approved by a bank for some reason and so they turn to other sources to find a loan. Working out a loan arrangement with someone can sound great - but it is a risky move. You don't have the same insurance and survivability as banks do and if someone refuses to pay you back, you are stuck with the loss. Providing loans as an investment opportunity should be carefully considered in all regards. I would recommend staying away from it. A type of loan I can see working favorably is owner-financing. This is where you own something such as a property and you sell it to someone, and you act as the bank. Instead of giving them money however, you give them the property or item they purchased. They make regular payments with interest and if they fail to make good on the debt, you are holding the item as collateral. If you are going to owner-finance something, make sure to do your research on it.

Bonds: A bond is a loan with a guarantee. Bonds tend to be some of the safest investments out of the traditionally advertised methods, especially when they are issued by the government. The problem with bonds is they lock up your money for a long time and the returns are very low. During the length of a bond the money being paid on the loan often doesn't even keep up with inflation. If the inflation rate in the U.S. is supposedly 1.4% and the interest paid to you per year on a U.S. government issued bond is 1.2%, then was any money made? The answer is no. There are types of bonds that advertise protection against inflation, but bonds in general will require a tremendous amount of money put into them to make any income as a return. Most individuals who buy bonds buy them as a safer investment to help balance out the risks they take in the stock market.

401(k): In its simplicity it is a special type of savings account that allows you to put in money, up to a certain amount each year, that isn't taxed at the time of deposit. It gets taxed later down the road whenever you decide to take the money out. The idea is that when someone decides to take their money out, they're at retirement age and not making as much income as earlier. With less income they pay less in taxes on the money when they finally withdraw it. The problem is that the money stays there for 30-40 years or more. Money in a 401(k) can be invested and used for stocks and such. If someone's income was at a high enough level that putting pre-tax dollars into a 401(k) would lessen their tax penalty to the point where their take-home pay was essentially unaffected, then it could make sense. Again, the downside is that money sits there for a long time out of your ability to use it. There are workarounds on this that people have come up with such as loans against it and such. Whether or not you use a 401(k) depends on your circumstances. I can see where it could be a fine idea, but I also see where it might just be following what the masses have told us to do for years. I wouldn't just do it because it exists, do the math on it and decide for yourself.

Buying things that reduce regular expenses: There is one more idea I want to mention. It is almost a backwards investment since it doesn't make you money but instead saves it. There are certain monthly expenses that can't really be avoided, and if someone had a surplus of cash they wanted to put somewhere - it could be of value to own the things that are normally costing money. Then they no longer have to be paid for. These are things like buying livestock (animals for food), setting up a small farm or garden, owning your home, etc. These things would need to be analyzed as per the chapters 8-10 and compared with other possible uses of your money. I can see several scenarios where it can make sense to make purchases that remove regular recurring costs

- such as your own food. An example is a friend of mine bought a cow, paid for it to be packaged and the meat delivered. This for him was a worthwhile investment as he is a big guy and spends a lot of money on food regularly. Doing this cost a chunk upfront but cut his expense for food significantly for most of a year and saved him a lot in the end.

For everything else let's keep it simple:

Put money into things that produce regular income.

Avoid putting money into things where the returns are speculative.

If you are looking at investments or investment opportunities, what category do they fit in? Will it be something that produces regular income, or will it be something that you buy at a certain price and hope that it will go up in value later?

Examples of things in the first category, things that produce regular income:
- Small businesses
- Online stores
- Real estate based on income vs speculative growth
- Owning things that reduce your monthly outgo as a sort of backwards investment
- Angel investing as described above
- Owner-financing a sale of something, such as a property

Examples of things in the second category, based on speculative returns:
- Stocks
- Mutual funds

- Other types of tradable funds, like exchange-traded funds (ETFs)
- Bonds
- Venture capitalism
- Real estate investments based on speculative growth
- Real estate investment trusts (REITs)

Personal loans fit more towards the first category, but I am leaving it off as an example because it can be very risky.

You probably noticed a common theme where the first category involves a more hands on approach and the second category is more in the direction of pay and sit back. The benefit of the hands-on approach is you have more input and control over the outcomes.

If I collected money for a long time in order to invest, I would not be happy about turning it over to other people to manage. I wouldn't want to give up control over it and its outcome.

CHAPTER 13: THE BANKER, THE LENDER, AND THE INVESTOR

What do these three have in common? They use money to make money.

But not in the sense that you or I would use money to make money - they use other people's money.

Sounds brilliant doesn't it? Collect and use other people's money in order to make themselves money. They limit the risk by using other people's hard earned and saved cash, not their own.

You need to understand these three. They control most of the money in the world and have a major influence on modern economics. In fact, the economy within the U.S. is the way it is due to people who are bankers, lenders, and investors. Some of this chapter might seem familiar or repeated data, but let's see where it goes.

Before diving in with number one - the banker, we are going to take a minute to look at how more money gets put into the U.S.

Recently, over $3,000,000,000,000 (3 Trillion) was injected into the U.S. economy. This is new money that didn't exist before. The money came from a bank called *The Federal Reserve*.

60-Minutes, the news show on CBS, interviewed the Chairman of The Federal Reserve Bank, Jerome Powell, just recently on this topic of the 3 Trillion new dollars and this is a direct quote from that interview:

INTERVIEWER: *"Where does it come from? Do you just print it?"*

CHAIRMAN: *"We print it digitally. So we, you know, as a central bank, we have the ability to create money. Uh, Digitally. And we do that by buying treasury bills or, or bonds, or other government guaranteed securities and that, that actually increases the money supply. We also print actual currency and we distribute that through The Federal Reserve banks."*

Ok, what does that mean? A few things.

First, the money is not issued by the U.S. government. It is issued by this bank called The Federal Reserve Bank, which is not part of the government. The bank is able to print dollars or add the numbers to their computer system, and like magic there is money. They put the money into circulation in the U.S. and they are given bonds in return. Remember from the definitions, a bond is basically a loan. This means they create the money out of thin air and then give it as a loan to the U.S. government and the people.

None of this is conspiracy or conspiracy theory. There is nothing secretive about this organization.

The U.S. government is in $27,000,000,000,000 (27 Trillion) of debt, which is an increase of $22 Trillion in twenty years (The debt was only $5 Trillion in the year 2000). The Federal Reserve is the bank that issues most of this debt.

Little exercise here: grab a dollar and look at it. See at the top it says, "Federal Reserve Note" What does *note* mean?

NOTE: another way of saying BANKNOTE, which means a piece of paper that represents a promise by the bank to pay the amount stated to the person holding the note on request.

It's a promise-note to pay you money. Now, you might think, *"But I thought it was money?"*

Well, if we go back in time a little bit, we see that gold used to be the main form of money. People traded in gold and gold was currency. Now, gold is heavy and hard to carry around with you. Some people were also worried about having a stash of gold in their house. They wouldn't want someone to break in and steal it.

Banks came around and advertised their purpose as a safe place to store your gold. You would take your gold that you had earned and bring it to the bank. They would take your gold and put it in their vault for safe keeping. They would then issue you a receipt for the amount of gold you deposited.

Now this receipt was important - it stated how much gold you stored and when. This receipt also acted as a promise that if you came back to the bank and presented it, they would give you your gold when you asked for it. This receipt is the note, or banknote. A promise that you will be repaid your gold.

Let's say you put the gold in and then later you wanted to buy something - you then would go back to the bank, exchange your note, and withdraw the necessary amount of gold from your account and then go make the purchase.

People knew that the bank would honor the note and issue the gold to whoever presented it. Because of this the notes had their own value and people started trading the notes instead of going through the process of withdrawing gold, paying for something, and having the other person re-deposit.

The notes were the money now.

In the United States in the past, the total amount of money in circulation represented the amount of gold held by the bank. You would in theory be able to approach the bank and withdraw an amount of gold equal to the amount on the notes you turned in. This system was known as "The Gold Standard."

On April 20, 1933, the President of the U.S. ordered all Americans to bring any gold they personally possessed to the Federal Reserve Bank and exchange it for notes. The gold was then stored at Fort Knox. If you have ever heard the expression "locked up tighter than Fort Knox" it is used because Fort Knox was obviously super secure due to holding all the gold. The President at that time (Franklin Delano Roosevelt) would not allow the private ownership of gold and ordered the entire gold supply of the U.S. be collected and secured.

By the beginning of the 1970's the U.S. came completely off the gold standard - meaning money no longer represented gold stored in the bank but was now just paper. It still had value and has value today since the people in the society believe in it and are willing to exchange it for other things, knowing they will be able to exchange it again later. A lot of people either forgot or never knew it used to be worth gold and only acted as a representation of gold.

Again, look at the dollar you have. If you don't have a dollar, look one up on your search-engine-of-choice's image results or go to: www.workingeconomics.com/resources-for-book-readers. See the "Federal Reserve Note?"

It's the same on British money. It is issued either by "Bank of England" or "The Royal Bank of Scotland." Look it up online, or visit the link above, if you don't have a 1-pound note near you.

In today's world, there is no currency that is still on the gold standard. In most cases and with most currencies people do not trade in paper notes but send numbers on a computer.

Now, back to The Federal Reserve Bank.

They are not part of the government but they have a government website: www.federalreserve.gov.

You can read up on what they have to say about themselves on their website. I don't think they are some evil organization here to drain the life and happiness of the American people, but it is worth knowing what they are and what they are about.

Now what about the smaller banks?

The Banker
He operates very similarly to how The Federal Reserve bank used to operate when we were on the gold standard as explained above, except instead of depositing gold you deposit hours worked or goods and services sold.

Wait. What?

The money you are putting into your bank account over at Bank of America doesn't represent ounces of gold but represents the 40 hours per week you worked the last 2 weeks. Or it represents 1,400 units of the product you sold.

You get this money that represents the value of what you gave for it, and you put it in your bank. The bank issues you a note, except now-a-days you just get numbers in your online banking account or bank app on your phone.

Banks provide almost no products or services that they sell or exchange to generate money. They really only make their money from the interest on loans, or from returns on investing money other ways.

Since they don't sell products to make any money, then where does the money come from to loan people and put into investments?

They use the money people have deposited for storage in their vaults.

The banker has an opposite point of view about money than you and I. They view money in their hands as a liability and they view loans to customers as assets. For a bank, money in their vault is a liability, since the people who deposited the money could come at any time and make a withdrawal - it also isn't making them any money just sitting there. There probably isn't a bank around that has enough money to issue to all its customers if they all came at the same time to empty their accounts. There is actually a name for this. It's called a "run on the bank" and can occur during times of extreme financial insecurity which causes people to lose faith in the bank. What do the banks do in such a time? They lock the doors.

Now, a loan is an asset for a bank - since it makes money for them. They get the money out of their hands and into the hands of borrowers who are then paying monthly interest and fees.

Some banks take the money deposited and instead of issuing it as loans use it to make investments.

What does the bank do with the money it makes from using their customer's money? It keeps it. The banks used to pay high interest to customers who kept their money in a savings account (at times 8% and even higher). At some point banks realized they didn't need to and now you find most savings accounts pay an interest rate of ½ a percent.

Banks generate insane amounts of profit from these activities.

There are also not-for-profit banks that are set up not to generate profit. But don't get the executives of one of these banks confused with the executive of your local nonprofit charity organization. The executives at these banks still *make bank* (make lots of money.)

The Credit Card Company
Credit card companies are banks. Most credit card companies are also attached to a bank or the credit cards are issued directly from a bank.

The average interest rate on credit cards right now is between 18-24%.

This interest rate is called APR - which stands for Annual Percentage Rate. This is the amount of interest paid per year while holding a debt on that credit card.

The math breaks down into monthly interest payments as follows: If you take an APR of 18%, and you divide that by 12 (for 12 months in a year) you get 1.5%. This amount of the total debt is paid monthly as interest. If the debt was $5,000, then each month $75 in interest is paid. Interest is paid in addition to the amount paid towards paying back the debt.

If you miss a payment you get an average late fee of $36.

Each month that there is interest or fees, they are added to the total debt. So, if they are missed again you pay interest on this new amount. It will grow forever if it isn't paid. An example of $5,000, where no monthly payments get made, will grow to $6,454 after 1 year. In 2 years, it will grow to $8,193. After 5 years, $15,731. In 10 years, the total debt that was never paid on would have grown to $41,951. This is an interesting example, but it never gets to that point. Before it gets that far there is a settlement made between the borrower and a collection agency, or the borrower gets sued and it's resolved in court.

18% returns per year is a great investment for any banker or investor. This is a big reason why many companies offer their own credit cards. Companies like: Amazon, Walmart, Target, Costco, Lowe's, Home Depot, and now Apple.

Credit card companies and banks that have customers who fail to pay back a loan are left with bad debt. Bad debt is a loss and so can be a write-off to lessen taxes owed on the profits of the credit card company.

Bad debts eventually get sold to collection companies for a fraction of the total debt. The collection companies then seek to get the full debt repaid to them from the borrower and use high pressure tactics to do so. Any amount they collect over the tiny price they paid for the debt is profit.

I'm not trying to paint this big evil picture of these banks or justify abandoning debt or not paying them back. But you should know who you are being indebted to. Some people also feel that they need to sacrifice things in their life to repay their debts. Well, don't live a crappy life to make the banks happy, but also don't incur debt you can't pay off. Look over the previous chapters on income, debts, and spending.

The Lender

There are other methods in which money is used to finance loans to people for the lender to make profits.

Payday loans are the worst of the bunch. The next worst would be getting a loan from the mafia because they will break your legs if you don't pay - like in the movies.

Different companies and industries extend lines of credit to customers and potential customers. This makes the selling of their goods or service easier for their customers as well as makes them more money than if they were just paid cash. Companies that extend credit or offer loans to finance a purchase would almost always prefer their customers to take the loan. They make much more money when they do. Why do you think the Home Depot or Macy's routinely offer you a credit card at checkout?

The car industry is huge at either providing their own loan options or having direct partnerships with banks or lenders that provide the loan. The car industry offers incentives and deals that guide the buyer towards using a loan. Most dealerships have "the back office" where the lender or finance guy sits. The lender is right there in the building.

Jewelry stores often do this. Their salesmen are trained to assume everyone coming in will want to use a loan to buy the jewelry and almost start the loan paperwork as part of the sales process.

Department stores do this too, such as Target.

They make more money when they loan to you, because you pay them more than just the cost of the product.

Offering a loan, or a payment-over-time option doesn't make the company evil. In fact, many times this allows someone to make a purchase when they wouldn't be able to without a loan. This is a valuable offering for many. When you are faced with the option of financing a purchase through the company, or their finance person, don't just take the loan because it is there. Consider your options as well as your ability to buy it in cash now or down the road.

The Investor

Here I am not referring to the normal person with some money in the stock market. I am talking about the big-time investor, the investment firm, financial advisors, money managers, etc.

Merrill Lynch is a big-time investing firm and money manager, and they are a branch of Bank of America. This is no secret as Bank of America customers often get offered Merrill Lynch products based on their account balances.

The investor is greatly benefited by the last hundred years of people being sold, continuously, on the need to invest. Investing seems confusing and hard to understand to a lot of people and so they seek out the professional.

The financial advisor collects the money from clients and invests it. They collect commissions, fees for trades, fees for assembling packages, and often a percentage of the fund for the year it's managed. Often the percentage is around 1%.

Charles Schwab is one of the larger such firms. They say they manage $3.56 Trillion. What would a 1% commission for managing $3.56 trillion be? It's $35,600,000,000 ($35.6

Billion) per year. That is a bit unfair because with a fund of this size the math is not so straight forward.

The big-time investor works with other people's money. Yes, there are people who use their own, but the real big-time investors collect and use other people's money to make investments.

The investor is not tied to the companies he invests in. He hopes the values of the investments go up, but the wellbeing of the company he invested in is only important if the market responds to it.

Many managing partners or members of boards of directors for companies feel they are the effect of their investors. They feel their value and worth is tied to the perceived value of the company in the stock market instead of the value of goods or services traded in the consumer market. They try to make the investors happy instead of the customers in many cases. This is why you, as a consumer, see big time companies make such stupid decisions that upset you and your friends - they are trying to make the investors happy. They're taking actions they believe will improve the perception of the company to investors.

The smart investor uses other people's money and if done right gets out with minimal backlash when there is a crash.

These investors move so much money that the small percentages add up to big time cash outs and massive paydays. The 4% your cousin made in stocks on his $40,000 of investments equals $1,600 - not much considering how much money was put at risk to make that $1,600. When the big-time investor makes 4%, it is made on $100,000,000 - so that 4% equals $4 Million.

These massive wins get talked about and filter down the line so the small guy sees how excited the big shots get on these 4% returns and thinks he should be happy on his $1,600 - even though he risked years of savings to get it.

There is little need to give these people your money. Most of the things they can do for you, you could do on your own. The professionals do have the ability to connect you with others and find opportunities, and they might have more familiarity than you. But, for the most part, these are all things you could learn and get on your own if you desired.

CHAPTER 14: WHAT IS RICH?

The answer to this question depends on who you ask. One study done by a big-time bank found that their customers thought having $2.3 Million in net worth is what it took to be considered wealthy.

Another study, done by a different group, found that their people would consider you rich if you make over $100,000 per year.

Either of those could be right, or both could be wrong - it depends on you.

I bet you've known someone who makes more than $200,000 a year and still has no money available to spend or save. You have probably met several people like this, but don't know it. If you don't think so, that's fine – I've known enough. You may also know people who seem to have very little money but are somehow always able to get what they need.

The level of income doesn't determine wealth. This is because in many cases people's quality of life matches or exceeds their income, and so they do not build any wealth. All their money is already used up, almost as if it is spent on expenses before it's even earned.

What would you consider rich? How would you measure it?

I believe it is important for you to know what you consider rich to be. Why? Well, wouldn't you like to be rich? Didn't you think about how cool it would be to be rich when you were a kid? Wouldn't you like to have an abundance of wealth? Almost everyone out there wants this and there is nothing wrong with that. Even the people who say things like "I just want enough to get by." They sure wouldn't mind having more money.

There is nothing wrong with money and having lots of it.

Having wealth is important to your ability to live and have the quality of life you want. Unexpected things happen in life and the safest guarantee to ensure you won't get messed up by freak, unplanned occurrences is to be wealthy. It is very desirable to have much more money than you need. Do you remember how much money there is out there in the world? There is nothing wrong in the slightest with you getting a good piece of that for yourself and keeping it.

If we need some sort of formula to figure out what would be rich for you, then let's use this simple math (note, the meaning of wealthy for you could be more than this number - if so then that's great!):

Take the total number in monthly income you need to generate (from what you worked out in Chapter 8) and multiply that by 3. Simple! If you get your monthly income up to that level, I would consider you rich.

Example: Your total number from the last step of Chapter 8 is $9,000. This multiplied by 3 is $27,000. Make that monthly and you would probably consider yourself rich.

CHAPTER 15: PERSONAL FINANCE

Personal finance is a hot topic. There are many online forums, communities, podcasts, videos, books, and other information sources on this topic.

Personal finance is a term used to mean things like managing your money, saving, investing, budgeting, banking, buying insurance, using mortgages, retirement planning, handling taxes, and managing your wealth.

You are not a business - you are a person. But you are an income producing entity and so the Laws of Economics apply to you. Many aspects of money management which apply to businesses apply to the individual as well.

I do however consider it of tremendous value for you to own a business, even if the business is made up of just you. There are too many perks for being a business owner not to be one.

If someone just follows the commonly spread or traditional advice on personal finance, they will have a life like the following example (warning, lots of numbers and math):

> Joe works at a small-time accounting firm. He makes $48,000 per year. He lessens his tax penalty by depositing 10% ($400 a month) into a 401k. After his 401k, taxes, Social Security, and any other government ordered fees, he receives $2,720 in his bank account each month - he lives in California. His wife Sally brings home another $2,000 monthly from

her self-employment income. This gives them $4,720 per month for their budget.

This allows them to spend $1,800 (30% of their pre-tax income) on housing. They purchased a house at a decent time in the housing market for $400,000. They got some help from their parents and made a down payment of $50,000. Their mortgage rate requires a monthly payment of $1,655.

Property tax for them works out to another $250 a month. They conserve where they can and so get their utilities bills down to $220 per month.

This adds up to $2,125 on housing. It is more than they're allowed per the 30% formula, but if they went any cheaper, they would end up in a different neighborhood than the one they wanted. Total remaining in their bank account after housing: $2,595.

Joe knows he is supposed to "pay himself first" and "pay himself 10%." He is already using a 401k to lessen his tax penalty, but he also wants to invest some money himself and so puts into his savings 10% every month. This equals $472. Total remaining: $2,131.

They're allowed 6% for groceries and 5% for eating out - this allows $519 for food between the two of them. Total down to $1,612.

They require internet service, phones, and TV. This adds up to another $242 based on average prices. Down to $1,370.

According to some sources, they are allowed 10-15% for car payments. This gives them $472 for cars at 10%, or $708 at 15%. They share one car and have a monthly payment of $391 on this car which they bought used. Their car insurance costs them $119, which is average. They don't drive too much and so only spend $100 on gas each month. They budget $98 for car maintenance to plan ahead - this covers what the average person spends on car maintenance per year. Magically, this total is $708 - which is 15% of their income figure. Total remaining: $662.

The average student loan payment is $393 per month. They each have student loans and so pay $786 per month. Total remaining: -$124.

They are supposed to budget $400 for home maintenance, but they can't afford to since they are already behind by $124 each month. Instead, if they need maintenance, they find the funds from other means or charge it on credit. Since they are following the common advice, they add this $400 to their monthly figure. Total: -$524.

They also have a little credit card debt which has a $124 minimum monthly payment. Total: -$648.

They are below their budget by $648 every month.

They don't have any money left over for fun stuff, but like most people they find a way and still go to the movies, take weekend trips, and have dinners and drinks with friends. Most of the extra expenses end up coming out of the "pay yourself 10% first" part of their budget or charged on credit.

They want to take more trips and vacations together but can't afford to.

They've talked about having kids but don't think they can afford it - they've heard people say that having a kid adds $1,000 to the monthly budget. Others have estimated a child will cost them over a million dollars by the time the kid reaches 18 years old. They try to follow the financial words of wisdom they've heard and feel guilty about wanting more than their budget allows.

Joe and Sally end up having one kid in their life together. They manage to make it work and luckily, they manage to keep their financial burden and stress away from their child's awareness.

Sally's income suffers a little as she decides to spend more time with their child to save on daycare - the average cost in their area is $800 per month. Overall, she manages to maintain about a $2,000 monthly self-employment income with only little dips here and there.

The company Joe works for is a stable firm and he works his whole life there. The stability of pay was too attractive to look elsewhere. He has friends who got laid off over the years and he is grateful for his steady job.

He eventually gets a promotion and more pay.

By the time they reach retirement age at 65, they have their house paid off. They've gone through several cars over the years, but now own two cars with the loans paid off.

According to financial blogs and 401k calculators - if all things went according to plan, they should have over a million dollars in their 401k. Most things don't go according to plan and the average 401k at retirement age is just under $200,000.

Joe and Sally got lucky, and since his employer had a 401k match program and the market performed favorably, for the most part, over 35 years they have a little under $700,000 in that 401k, after a lifetime of work and saving.

They do the math and figure out that if they live frugally (without spending a lot) and on only $30,000 a year (or $2,500 per month), they should be able to stretch this out the rest of their lives. Unfortunately, due to inflation over their lifetime, that $30,000 per year doesn't buy what it did when they started their lives together.

In fact, according to current inflation estimates, in 30 years $30,000 will have the same value that $14,301 has today. This means that their retirement would be like trying to live on $1,191 per month today, not $2,500 like they thought when they made their plans.

Is this story depressing to you? It was depressing for me to write it. The names are fictional, but this pattern is sort of "The American Dream" in application. This is the direction people are taught to go.

For Joe and Sally, you can say they were a "success" since they got to retire at 65. But the cost was a cheap life and a cheap retirement. They never planned for what they wanted. They followed the pattern taught to them and handled their finances in reaction to the other factors in their life. They never took charge to make the life they wanted. Maybe they were sold that the life they got was desirable, when it really wasn't what they wanted. What they actually wanted was to have more kids, a bigger and better house, more vacations, more fun. But they gave all that up and stuck to the advice of experts.

I have talked with quite a few people about their personal finances. Commonly, people get confused when they find their income has gone up and they don't have any more money to show for it. People talk about following the advice of the blogs and podcasts and how they have been warned about "lifestyle creep" - meaning their lifestyle expenses slowly getting bigger over time.

The people following these pieces of advice fail to notice that the same people telling them to watch out for increased expenses, also give them the same advice that causes their expenses to go up. What? They advise only 30% for housing and 20% for such and such. What happens when their income goes up? When their income goes up, the amount that equals 30% of their income also goes up. They have more available for housing and other things - so they spend more. They are still following the same financial advice as before and are spending more as a result.

This is the result of reactionary budgets or making your budget and modifying your expenses as a reaction to your changing income levels.

Now, I do get that the guidance of "just go make more money" is lacking in understanding, but that is really what it takes to win at personal finance. The principles of how to do it are within the other chapters of this book. The whole book contains a working understanding on the subject of personal finance - so there is no additional direction here in this chapter.

I just gave you the story of the normal. And what I would consider an unfulfilled financial life. I'm not giving you an example or story of success in personal finance, because as cheesy as this might sound: *that is your story to write.*

CHAPTER 16: BUSINESS FINANCE

The subjects of personal finance and business finance are covered throughout this book. But they are both hot topics which is why we are going over them specifically. Since there are differences between personal and business finance, each gets their own chapter.

Like in earlier chapters, let's go over the *normal*, and what I would consider unsatisfying:

Emily is a small business owner. Her business makes custom tables for various other businesses including coffee shops, art galleries, hotels, poker rooms, and more.

She has two full-time employees and one part-time that help with the making of the custom tables, and a part-time employee to help with administrative functions.

Her business account goes up and down but tends to hover around $9,000.

She manages to regularly pay her employees on time, barely. But she doesn't pay herself what she is worth.

She gets a down payment on an order of tables. She uses this money to pay the rent for her shop, and a little of it on her website fees. She is hoping she can collect the balance of the payment by the end of the month so she can pay her staff without having to take funds from the $9,000 in her business account.

The end of the month comes near, and she doesn't collect the remaining payment on the order. She has to use some of her $9,000 to pay her 4 staff, but she is unable to pay herself this month.

Her payment is due for her small business loan she used when she got started, she got a really good deal and so her monthly payment is only $2,000.

After the payments and the end of the month passes, she collects the remaining balance on the recent job. She gets another order from a previous customer but doesn't have enough for the materials. She thinks about getting another loan to fund this. She has to purchase the materials but decides she doesn't want to get another loan and so uses money from her own personal bank account to buy the materials.

She is stressed out every day and working overtime with next to no pay and hoping for some good luck.

This story uses a small business - but the finances of big business, with hundreds of employees or more, are often run in a very similar way.

What we're about to go over isn't everything on business finance, but these points in addition to the earlier chapters cover a lot of it.

The points below also happen to be the missing ingredients in this story of Emily the table maker, and are also missing in many other businesses today:

Every bit of money gets allocated

This is of massive importance. Ensure all money received is allocated, meaning that you should decide on what all of it will be used for. How to spend it is in the chapter on spending. From Economic Law #10: *Money that is not allocated will eventually disappear. People and businesses find a way to spend more than they make and so unallocated money will eventually get spent.*

To avoid money apparently disappearing, or sprouting legs and running away, you consciously and intentionally spend it and decide where it goes. If you or your business wants to have a "slush fund" or "petty cash," meaning an amount of money for random or unplanned expenses, then that is no problem. Just intentionally allocate for a slush fund instead of making your whole account balance the slush fund.

Any money not allocated and separated from just a pile of money in the account is at risk. To ensure your money isn't at risk of disappearing or being spent on less than needed expenses, you make sure that every bit is allocated and accounted for, down to the penny.

Decide where your money goes so it doesn't appear to decide on its own.

Sequence of priorities for spending

Not all expenses are the same. Different things might have the same cost to you, but they provide different values in return. For example: Paying employees to continue to work is more important than repaying a business loan or debt. I'm not saying don't pay the debts, but if the employees don't get paid and walk off from the job, then you can't make any more money.

The sequence for your priorities is laid out in Chapter 8, but here they are again with a slant towards your business:

1. *Have an understanding of what it costs to operate and make more than that. This includes the cost for sales, marketing, and finding work to do.*

2. *Allocate for future income producing needs. Make funding future income production as important as funding the cost to operate.*

3. *Have reserves to fund specific future opportunities or potential needs, including a reserve to handle disasters.*

4. *Have a plan to address debt and stick to it. Don't incur debt without a plan for handling it as well. Paying debt has a much lower priority than other business expenses. Try to avoid debt and get the business to fund itself.*

5. *Factor in all things that you need and desire to spend money on - EVERYTHING. Total these costs and set this as your do or die number. You have to get income to this level and can't rest until you do. Don't budget reactively but plan how to spend your money before you make it.*

Fund the cost to deliver with each sale or service & always make a profit

A lot of businesses look at how much money they have at the end of the month and then decide what is going to get funded. There is a system of financial management in use at many businesses of using the money gained from Job Number 2 to pay off what remains on the delivery cost from Job Number 1. They then use some of the money earned from Job Number 3 to pay for Job Number 2, and so on.

This brings about a need to dip into reserves, savings, or incur debt.

Too many individuals and businesses do this. Talk with another business owner and you might learn that he or she is clueless as to how the finance people of the company manage the money and expenses. Or you could learn that he or she knows what is happening and is in a state of disbelief about it - but doesn't know what to do or doesn't even try to change anything. In some cases, the reasoning is, "Well, that's how we've always done it..."

Talk to the finance people in the same company and learn the same thing in reverse. They are confused why the boss makes them handle money this way. Why can't they fund a project with the same money earned for doing the project?

Even worse, there are times when businesses deliver goods or services at a loss. The cost to deliver is not understood and so each job ends up costing them instead of earning money for the company. Even worse still, are the businesses that operate at a loss intentionally, thinking it will be made up down the road somehow or from some other department within the company.

Each department or unit within a company should be fully capable of funding itself. If it isn't funding itself then what is the point in having it? If it cannot be figured out for a department or unit to pay for itself then there is a problem. It is relying on the other parts of the company, or your savings to stay alive. With lack of a better way to put it: it is a leech sucking the life and finance away from the parts that earn it and should be dealt with quickly. This is not to say that something like the personnel department should be selling things or doing the delivery of the company in order to fund its activities. But it should be providing enough services within the company to be worth more than the cost to keep the department.

Now, there are of course positions that are vital to ensuring future income but may not have an obvious up-front return. This needs to be remembered when doing an assessment. A position like an administrative assistant might not have the obvious returns that a salesperson has, but the freed-up time made available for an executive by having an assistant is likely worth several times the cost of the salary.

There are other potential examples where the returns or value gained doesn't occur until later on. Such a possible example is social media marketing. It might not give you money the day you pay for it, but it will likely create future interest that can later generate sales.

When money gets allocated to pay for the cost of delivery - it should get sent out in short order. Don't wait for the bill to come all the way up to the due date for expenses that were necessary to deliver. Doing so allows the money to sit longer, opening up the possibility of you or someone else deciding the money could actually go to something else. It's better not to carry a balance on the things necessary to deliver goods and services. It is better to pay these bills when they can be paid and not let them stack up.

To handle these things is simple. For each job that is sold you:
1. Count up the cost to deliver the work including all things that require money. Things like transportation, hours of employee work, materials, tools, etc.
2. If the total cost to deliver is more than the amount of money to be gained, then something needs to change. Either the cost needs to be reduced, the price needs to increase, or the work needs to be not done. There are certain circumstances such as resolving an upset customer or fixing a messed-up job where this doesn't apply, and you pay the loss in order to keep a favorable relationship with a client or customer

base. Many things can reduce costs to deliver, including training employees better.

3. When the money is received it is first used to pay for the delivery, everything remaining then goes to the company and is allocated per the second priorities and on as above under *Sequence of priorities for spending.*

Separate your bank accounts

Many get into the habit of collecting the income into one account and then spending for things as they are needed from the same account. Some have 1 bank account and 1 savings. Some even just use their own personal bank accounts and don't have anything specifically set up for the business. All of these can be mistakes.

When all the money goes into the same account, it can be difficult to determine what funds are for what purposes. This can be resolved by using spreadsheets that account for every dollar, or by having different accounts for different types of reserves or allocations, or a mixture of both.

You can use different accounts for different types of expenses, or credit cards that are paid off each month on different types of purchases, or whatever method that can make a separation of funds easier for you.

It is definitely important to have your own personal bank account separate from the business. How else are you to get paid if there is no account to send the money to? *WHAT?! Get paid? That's crazy...*

Pay yourself as the owner

If you aren't making any money, then what's the point? Many people who own a business undergo and experience more stress than the average employee. The owner has more responsibilities, deadlines, payments to make, etc. Why wouldn't they deserve some pay?

Sacrificing your own pay to "reinvest" back into the company can bring up images of walking on a treadmill - moving without actually getting anywhere, at least in terms of personal pay. If you can't get the company to produce enough income to pay for itself and also pay you, then it's likely to continue needing the money you are denying yourself in order to keep going.

If the company relies on your salary to operate, how can it ever function if you decide to take your salary back?

You need to pay yourself from your business and you need to pay yourself well - otherwise what's the point?

Reinvesting in your company

In addition to paying yourself, you need to fund future ideas, projects, tests, etc. This should be funded as part of your allocations under the *Sequence of priorities for spending*, but it is worth a little extra comment here for importance.

Reinvesting in your own company should not be boiled down to just sacrificing salary to pay for operations. This is operating at a loss and is not what I am talking about.

You need to build up an opportunity fund for your business in order to fund experimental projects and new ideas. Very few business owners don't come up with new ideas or things they want to try out. The mistake is to change course and direct the energy and efforts into this new idea. The right way would be to have some funding available to stand up a test project and see the workability of it before making it a permanent fixture within the company.

This fund to pay for experimental or trial projects is what I mean by reinvesting in your company. You might not have something in mind to fund right now, but have some money stashed for when you do. It's almost inevitable to have new ideas as you interact with the market more and more and learn of more demands people have that aren't being met adequately or at all.

Taxes and legal

Never avoid taxes and never operate illegally.

Always pay taxes and on time. Always have your legal bases covered.

And always document the fact that you are in compliance and have the records to prove it.

Doing these things makes you bulletproof. Failing to do them opens the door to getting shut down or indebted to the government. There is no substitute for an understanding of taxes and legal. Yes, it is perfectly all right to hire professionals, but there is no substitute to understanding it yourself.

Failing to understand these subjects opens you to more risk than necessary. You become totally reliant on the legal professionals and accountants. If they were wrong about something how would you know? If they were stealing, how would you know? If they were steering you in the wrong direction how would you know?

It pays high returns to at least have enough knowledge for you to understand what the pros you hired are doing, and also to be able to inspect your own financial records and legal status. You don't need to go to college for 7 years but read some books or do some internet searching.

Sales

There is so much data out there on the subject of sales. Sales is considered the life force of many companies. Many other companies ignore sales completely - relying solely on their marketing efforts.

There is a distinction between sales and marketing. Marketing gets the customers and gets them interested. Sales gets them to buy. Yes, there are many successful marketing efforts that result in the purchases of goods and sales made, but without a sales team with personal contact to prospective buyers there are sales being missed.

Many prospects require a personal contact to help them get over the indecision or fear of making a purchase, and so without a sales staff these people don't buy, or they end up buying much, much later. It's because of this missing ingredient in many companies that marketers will tell you that a purchasing rate of 1% is a good ratio. They skip over that they were marketing to a targeted audience that has already expressed interest in this market. There is already a demand waiting to be met with the people they are marketing too. What about the other 99%? Do they not deserve the product too?

Marketing can generate a lot of the income necessary for a company to survive, but using sales is what makes explosive growth possible. I'm not cutting short marketing here at all. I am boosting the importance of sales.

Marketing is vital, and per Law #14: *Without marketing, there will be no business. The more potential buyers within your market that know of you, of your supply, and think of you - the better off you will be.*

Let's also not forget Economic Law #15: *Sales is the bridge between Marketing and the purchase. Without a sales staff or system, purchases of a product are being lost.*

Records of previous customers

Most big companies know that the previous purchasers are the biggest source of future income. This is a true datum: People who have bought before can and do buy again.

Some big companies make it hard to quit their service, and others offer a reward for you to stay and not leave them. Most cable companies are like this. They make it hard to cancel or make a decent effort to keep you if you call to cancel service.

It is so important to keep your records of who has bought what from you, when they bought it, their contact information (all of it), and any other relevant or important information.

Even if you don't have any other product to offer them at the time of a sale, or the product they got is a one-time purchase only - still collect the info. Sometime down the road it is likely you may have another product or service offering, and this customer already knows you and has already paid you money and has done business with you. They are a good prospect for your future service, even if the future service is not yet available.

One of the main reasons big companies buy other companies is to get their records and lists of previous customers. They are then able to sell and provide services or products to this newly expanded customer base.

Quality

If you deliver a crappy product or service or give someone who paid you money less than what they expected, your business is at risk.

If you went to a nice restaurant and were greeted lifelessly by the host, asked to wait for a table, and not offered a place to sit but had to stand awkwardly at the entrance, you'd already be telling yourself the food better be worth it. You look around and see there are tables obviously available, but you are made to stand there waiting a little bit anyway. Even though you are the only person waiting, the bored host calls out your last name and waits a second for a response. Then you are taken to a table in the back by the kitchen exit.

You sit and look at the menu and within moments decide you want the burger. It is expensive for a burger, but it looks tasty. You are waiting for the waitress to come take your order. You can see multiple servers by the cash register whispering to each other, obviously gossiping. After what seems like a long time you grab one of the guys cleaning the tables and ask if you can give your order. He says he can't, and you need to wait for your server.

Eventually, your waitress shuffles over, trying to hide her bad attitude. Underneath her forced smile you see the obvious expression of annoyance that she was pulled away from her conversation, or her phone. She opens her mouth and with a dulled voice tells you the day's special, it's as if it was the hundredth time she said it that day. You order the burger, and she walks away.

After another twenty minutes your burger comes out. It is not at all what you expected. It is small, way over cooked, quickly tossed together, and the buns are soggy. You don't even finish eating it. You think about getting up and just walking out or asking to talk to the manager - but decide it isn't worth it and just pay and leave.

On the way out the host sort of whispers like a faint recording on repeat, *"Thanks for coming by, we hope to see you again."* Yeah right!

Will you ever want to go through that again? That wasn't a meal - it was a horror sideshow at a carnival.

You will probably never go to that restaurant again. They lost a customer for life. You will probably recommend to all your friends, family, and associates to stay away. You might even register an account on a review website to share the awful experience and leave a 1-star review.

Get the point? These are errors in quality.

Reverse the whole story - and you have an amazing experience and a delicious meal. You would be happy to give a 5-star review, recommend this place to everyone you know and return many, many times.

Quality is incredibly important. Different degrees of quality impact your word-of-mouth, repeat business, and ability to stay profitable. Always deliver good service and excellent products.

Debts and outside capital
Using debt when it can be avoided, or outside capital, opens you up to risk. A business is an income producing entity and if it is unable to fund an expense with its own production and management of funds, then the expense is either: A) Not needed, or B) There is something else wrong.

The lack of money is very, very rarely the actual problem. But it is very, very commonly the blamed reason for a failure. It is the obvious one, yet somehow when outside money is gotten it often doesn't resolve the overall scene, and other things still require funding, or there are other fires that need to be put out.

Applying all the principles in this book should set you up to never need outside funding, and you will probably laugh at the idea of selling off pieces of your company to get some cash.

Marketing

Marketing is how new customers get found. Without new customers there is no future. An existing customer base will eventually dry up and run out of money or demand. If a customer base was very large it might take a long time, but eventually it will disappear - so will the company.

New customers need to be constantly added to the customer base. New prospects need to be found and more and more people need to be made aware of the company and the service or product offering. Marketing is the section of the business that does this. Marketing needs to be treated with importance and adequately funded and staffed.

Some people rely on the efforts of outside companies for marketing services. There is nothing wrong with using professionals, but similar to how there is no substitute to knowing legal and taxes, there is no substitute to understanding marketing and having someone within your company responsible for the marketing efforts - even if it's you.

Totally outsourcing marketing can sound attractive, cheaper, or the right thing to do - but don't do it. Marketing drives the customers to you and allows you to make the money, don't forget that. Markets and marketing are important and get their own chapter, and it's coming up next.

CHAPTER 17: MARKETS AND MARKETING

Marketing is another topic with many, many podcasts, books, etc. We will cover some of the basics. Each one of these points below could be a whole chapter or book in itself, so we will only be going over them briefly.

MARKET: A particular area of interest where similar goods and services can be classified together and where there is exchange of money for these types of goods and services. Examples would be the laptop computer market, real estate market of San Francisco, or the real estate market of Milwaukee, WI, or the fine art market of Northern Seattle. There can also be sub-markets within markets. For example, the business laptop market, within the laptop market, or the luxury homes market within the San Francisco real estate market.

MARKETING: Promoting and selling products or services, doing market research, getting materials to potential buyers to inform them of a product or company and advertising. It is getting customers to want the services or goods and wanting to buy them.

Finding markets

Markets are not hard to find, but you need to know how to look for them. The first thing to follow is a demand. If a demand exists, and there is something to supply to those with the demand and it is supplied, then there is a market. Remember there needs to be an exchange of money for there to be a market. Just people wanting things doesn't translate to money being made in that industry.

There has to be a demand, and a recognition that they can get a product to fulfill their demand.

Example: The Democratic Republic of the Congo in Africa, has one of the largest supplies of diamonds. The people who live there make less than $400/year on average. The order of importance for these people would put diamonds way, way down at the bottom of their list of expenses. The only value the average person there sees in diamonds would be to sell to someone else to get money in order to buy the things needed to live. They would have less interest in wearing a diamond ring, necklace, or earrings. Yes, there are rich people in the Congo, but does that mean there's a market to sell diamonds too? There isn't. The rich people there are probably in the industry of exporting goods themselves, including diamonds. In fact, the purchase of diamonds across all of Africa is so low it isn't counted by most sources who report on the global diamond trade. Here we have one of the largest supplies in the world, and at the same time one of the lowest demands.

To find potential markets, locate demands. If you find a group or classification of people with a demand, and there is an exchange of money for products to meet their demand - you have found a market.

If you identify a need or demand for something and there are no trades to satisfy it, then you have found a *prospective* market, or a market you could create and develop. It does not mean there is success guaranteed, just that it can become a successful market.

Finding existing markets and submarkets to sell products to is easier and more surefire than trying to develop a new market.

However, the companies that develop a new market completely own that market and almost all the money it generates. Example of such a developed market is the Microsoft Office collection of software like Word and Excel. Another example is PayPal.

Instead of just looking for collections of people, and instead of "looking for what pains people," follow the demand. See if there is an exchange of money for a product to meet that demand and see if there is some aspect you can better satisfy or supply. Find out who are the people and/or organizations that are spending money here and find out where they are going to look at or learn more about available products. This is sort of a formula to finding markets. It can apply to industries, locations, etc.

Additionally, someone would have an easier time following the above paragraph and developing a product or service to satisfy a demand versus envisioning a product or service and then trying to find a market for it. This is because there is already an existing demand. Developing a product first does not mean there will be a demand for it.

A demand without an exchange of money is not a market, it is just a demand.

The value of an identified market as a whole
$26 Billion spent on birdwatching, $3 Billion for bags of ice, $62 Billion on cosmetics like makeup, $2 Billion on chewing gum, $80.5 Billion on the lottery, $31 Billion goes to buying flowers, $2.4 Billion buying hotdogs from the store.

To find the value of the market and whether a product or service offering can generate profits you have to actually look at the value generated as a market - not the individual purchaser.

If a pack of hotdogs cost $5, and someone only bought two packs then that is only $10. $10 is not a lot of money. But the market for hotdogs purchased in stores within America generates $2.4 Billion per year.

On the reverse side, if someone sold obscure paintings of strange images of dead birds by the non-famous, French artist Jean Piere-lu Ricard Bleu for $100,000 a piece (don't look it up, it's not real), and there was only 1 person ever interested in those paintings, then that is a tiny market. That market only generates $100,000.

To see the value of a product or service and how much money it can make, you have to look at the market it fits into and how much money is there currently being exchanged. The money that exists in that market is the money you will be tapping into and that's the pie you are taking a slice out of.

At the same time, looking at where else the money is going within that market reveals your competitors, or potential competitors. Competitors are not only the companies that have the same product offering as you, or even a similar one. Competitors are also those that compete to capture some of the money in a particular market - this is called market share.

Without forgetting the individual customer, look at the market, see where the money is going and why.

Reaching markets

Similar to seeing the value by looking at a market instead of just looking at individuals - you reach the market by communicating... to the... you guessed it... the market. You study the individuals and look for common patterns and common decisions or purchasing reasons, but then you send your marketing materials to the collective people in that market.

If you only focus on chasing down individuals to market to and make sales, then you only get those people. You miss out on the potential of the larger market. Don't forget the individual, but also don't forget the market.

By directing marketing efforts to your market, you reach more customers and potential customers. Almost as if the words *market* and *marketing* have something to do with each other.

Example: The small-time construction company only markets to individual homeowners and their friends directly. They send them mail directly or ask previous customers for referrals. The big-time construction company got a list of all real estate agents, investors, as well as homeowners - and sends them marketing materials regularly.

Another important aspect is making sure your marketing efforts are going to the right market. This is the market you have identified for your product or service offering. You could send all the marketing material that exists about diamonds to the people of the Congo, but it's not going to generate sales. You can send all the marketing material on credit card consolidation loans to billionaires, but none of them are interested. You can send a little bit of marketing materials on your supply of truffles (a rare and expensive edible fungus served in expensive restaurants) to fancy restaurants and have tremendous success.

Marketing is for the market. Sales is for the individual.

Types of marketing channels

A channel is a route for communication or information to travel on. There are three broad classifications for marketing channels:

1. Pre-existing channels that are owned or controlled by others
2. Channels you own or develop for new customers
3. Channels you own or develop for people who know you

One: Pre-existing channels that are owned or controlled by others

Most markets have many of these. These channels can be owned or controlled by other companies, fans of the services or the industry itself, the purchasers of products, distributors, etc. The benefit of these is that they already exist, and they already have people there who are interested, and with an existing demand.

These could be anywhere that people with shared interests or demands gather together to talk about their interests, or to receive information. This can be in person, printed publications, over the internet, etc. Examples of such channels would be podcasts, YouTube channels, social media influencers, internet forums, talk shows, magazines, blogs, newsletters, conventions, and much more.

To find an existing channel simply get this question answered: *Where are the people in this market going for information? Or, where are they receiving their information from?*

To successfully utilize an existing channel normally costs you either A) Money, or B) Time invested to gain trust or build yourself as an authority with the people there. This is most often in online forums and communities. Or C) Get another authority, or the owner/controller to promote or communicate on the channel for you (normally requires money or something else in return).

Two: Channels you own or develop for new customers
These consist of ways for you to get your information and marketing materials to new people. These channels could be things like YouTube videos, blog posts, guest blogging, podcast episodes, using previous customers for referrals, other businesses referring, etc.

You own these channels, or you develop them. It doesn't require you to exchange money with people outside your own company to take advantage of. The downside is if you haven't developed it already then these can take time. It is smart to have your own channels as it is not hard to make them in the modern world, but it can take time to build up their ability to reach people in volume.

Three: Channels you own or develop for people who know you
This is a different channel than the one for new customers. In most cases you won't be offering the same goods or services in the same way to new customers as you would to previous customers or people who know you. Sometimes it doesn't matter. But in most businesses, these require different marketing materials and different messages. This is because the previous customer already knows you, or at least knows you better, and so you don't have to explain yourself.

There are many ways you can communicate, interact, and market to people who know you. This is a vital channel to have and maintain as there is a lot of money in this portion of your market. Use things like emails, email lists, twitter, Facebook, Instagram, other social media, letters, postcards, phone calls, etc.

People have had success with only using one of these classifications of channels and ignoring the others. However, using all three ensures you reach the highest number of people and continue reaching the highest amount possible. From Economic Law #14: *The more potential buyers within your market that know of you, of your supply, and think of you - the better off you will be.*

Strengthening demand

This can be done through manipulation and shady, dishonest means. I'm going to skip over those ways, but if you really wanted to know for yourself you can look over which of the Laws affect demand and I'm sure you can think of some ways that demand can be manipulated dishonestly.

To strengthen a demand, you must have first identified a demand, found a market, and found the people that make up that market. You must also have found a channel in which to communicate your information to potential customers within the market. By highlighting the benefits and improvements to their quality of life, their demand can be strengthened.

Demand for a product can be developed through marketing efforts by showing the product and its qualities, instead of just showing things about the company that offers it. This works best when you dominate a market share. When you dominate a market share you should promote the product and product category itself, not just your business.

If you don't dominate a market share you promote your company or name in alignment with the exact demands you meet, or the reasons you found that get people to buy these types of products.

Strengthening the specific demand for *your* offering, instead of someone else's, is best done by improving the quality of your offering and the friendliness in which it is delivered.

Word of mouth, which is people promoting you to their friends on their own, is the most effective marketing there is. Doing things to increase word of mouth also increases demand for *your* offering. Some things you can work on to boost word of mouth are: increasing quality, consistency, friendliness, better communications, meeting or exceeding expectations, and faster service.

Creating a new demand for your product

You might have a scenario where you don't think there is a demand for your product or an existing demand within your market. I would say look further. It is quite possible there is an existing demand, and it was missed.

If for some reason you cannot find a demand, and you have some product that you want to sell and deliver then you will need to create the demand.

Some people might not yet have a demand for your particular product, or type of product, because nothing like it existed before. Since it didn't exist before, there was nothing to be marketed to generate or strengthen demand for it. Sometimes such a product comes into being, and when people learn about it, they can't get it fast enough. An example would be the creation of smart phones. The Apple iPhone wasn't the first "smart phone," but it was the first product to fit what we now know as smart phones. It entered into a market of flip-phones, where actual internet and apps didn't exist. No one knew they would want Instagram or Twitter on their phone, because it didn't exist - until it did. Now there is enough smart phones sold to supply nearly half the population of the planet.

The easiest way to create a demand is to find an existing one in a nearby or complimenting market and identify the points that generate that demand. What do the people in that market buy and what motivates them to buy it.

I said a nearby market, so the market and products you examine must align with your product and the new market you will be developing. The products you examine must have a demand that your product can also compliment or contribute to.

You can promote to these people within that market using existing marketing channels. You can promote how your product can complement the other product or products they already have a demand for.

You can find parts of a demand that aren't being fully satisfied, and then do marketing which describes how you address those specific parts. This can accelerate the creation of a new demand and a new market rapidly.

Example: OxiClean (something added to laundry detergent for increased cleaning power) was a brand-new product in 1997. It isn't a laundry detergent and doesn't compete with other detergents. You use it *with* detergents. They successfully created a massive demand for this product by identifying a demand for clean, stain-free clothing and marketed heavily on that point. They showed that you use it *with* detergent and so there was no competition with existing products. They created a market and instantly dominated it. Other similar products might have existed before, but OxiClean built up this market and owned it.

Another way to create demand is to highlight the features of your offering and the problems it solves, benefits it grants, advantages it gives, and what is returned to the person for spending their time or money on it. You promote these things using existing channels to people identified as potential buyers.

One more on developing a demand, also the simplest and most powerful: Learn what the people you are going to market and sell to demand. Figure out how your product does or gives those things that satisfy their demand. Then find ways to communicate that your product does or gives those things.

Guiding the market to YOUR product

The best way to guide people to your product over other offerings is to appear to be everywhere. If you were to work out all the possible marketing channels from the three broad classifications above, and then market on all of them effectively and consistently, you would win.

The trick is to market on these channels enough to get your target audience to keep you in mind, but not so much that you oversaturate this channel or become annoying. If someone is seeing your same ad multiple times a day on each social media platform, on YouTube, in their email inbox, and others and this is going on every day for weeks that person would get annoyed and might actually begin to reject your offering.

You need to work out what is the ideal amount of advertising for your customer and your market to make sure they get your materials just enough that they don't forget about you.

Once you've got that worked out, you need to do it and do it consistently. You also need to keep a finger on the pulse of this, meaning watch how it is performing and any relevant feedback and adjust accordingly.

When you have someone to service, deliver the best services or goods possible with high quality and friendliness.

One additional point is to have salespeople, or at least have sales as its own function worked out for your product or offering. There needs to be an incoming channel set up to receive people and their requests when they are interested, want more information, or haven't yet decided on their own that they want to make the purchase. Having some way for the people who haven't yet decided between your product or the competition's product to contact you, get more data and get sold, is critical to your success.

Making the purchase as easy as possible

This is a commonly missed part of a sales process, especially where products are sold online. The less decisions that need to be made by a possible buyer, or the less actions they need to take to make the purchase, or the less paperwork and discussions they need to have, the better.

This part isn't about getting them to want to buy, it's about letting them actually hand over the money once they decided to make a purchase.

In a near perfect system, when a possible buyer decided to make a purchase, he would then only need to click one button, or swipe a credit card, or hand over money right then and there.

Certain industries need contracts signed or forms filled out. Sometimes it is unavoidable and necessary for legal protection. In these situations, limit the paperwork as much as possible, and the amount of forms that need to be filled out before payment is received. Shorten the process without forgetting any legal requirements.

Every time a possible buyer needs to take another action, or make another decision, or fill out another form, or complete any other step on the way to making the purchase (that is paying the money), the chances of them changing their mind increase.

Each additional step is another opportunity for the buyer to think about it, or to change his or her mind.

Last year $4 Trillion dollars worth of online shopping carts were abandoned.

The massive online store Amazon learned this early and uses a one-click buy button. They removed the need for us to sort through a large collection of sellers or sources of product. Imagine deciding you wanted to buy a new sweater for your dog. After much shopping you picked the one you wanted on Amazon. Then you had to sort through all of the sellers and pick the seller you wanted to buy from. You don't know who any of these people are! You know Amazon, but you don't know *Dogs Sweaters Plus,* or *Dogs Need Clothes Too Inc.* You would have to sort through all of these, check their reviews and ratings, and check out which one you trust the most and which one has the best price. You would also need to see what they calculate for shipping costs, or if they ship for free. Each step of this process is another chance for you to change your mind.

Amazon simplified it and made it so you just click "Buy." They do all the deciding for you behind the scenes. They do this so well that most people have no clue that Amazon is actually a marketplace for other companies, and a lot of the time you buy something you are actually buying from some other company.

Sometimes buyers have fear or uncertainties or doubts when they want to make a purchase, and so you want to limit the amount of time they have to fight with their fears, uncertainties, or doubts.

For another way to make the purchase easier: limit the choices. If someone wanted to buy coffee from your online fancy coffee store, and they click the "I want to buy your coffee right now" button and were taken to a list of 45 choices they would be unable to complete the purchase then and there. They would have to now research and read up on all the options. It is fine to have a large inventory, but in this example you should probably highlight a "First time buyer" recommendation, a "Try something new" recommendation, or a "Most popular choice."

Another way to make it easier is to have as many possible paying options as possible, such as all major credit cards, PayPal, etc.

I used a lot of online examples, but this is just as important in a person to person sale as well. In a car dealership if the buyer has to go through and turn 99 pages and sign each one, that is 99 times he could suddenly decide he actually better go home and talk it over with the wife first.

Yet another point is when a face-to-face or over the phone sale is being made and the person wants to pay - stop talking and take the money. You can always continue talking afterwards, but when someone is ready to give you money and you don't accept it, they might change their mind. It's perfectly fine if someone changes their mind, but if someone is experiencing fear, uncertainty, or doubt on purchasing your product, don't contribute to their fear, uncertainty, or doubt by making them sit in it longer.

A final one for this section: Make sure you or your salespeople can and will actually offer the sale and ask for the money. Some people are not able to ask for money and so they rarely ask, and as a result they rarely make any money as a salesperson. Something as simple as "Would you like that dog-sweater gift wrapped?" or even as basic as "Would you like to make a purchase?" can be the difference between making a sale or not.

Getting the product delivered

When the sale is made, ship the item right then and there.

When the contract is signed get them scheduled for delivery immediately.

When the money is handed over, hand them what they paid for.

When the check clears, start delivering the service.

Don't wait until next week. Don't wait until tomorrow. Don't even wait until the later part of the day - do it now.

This can be a hard thing to pull off, but it increases success massively. Instant delivery is one of the best ways to protect against someone changing their mind and asking to undo the sale or to get a refund.

Getting the customer what they wanted, when they wanted it, makes them happy. And when did they want it the most? When they decided to pay for it!

You might not think you are able to get your delivery done instantaneously, but you can at least schedule it right then and there. This is something people in business should continually improve on and work to maintain.

Spend money on your marketing

You have to spend money on marketing. You need to constantly allocate for it. It is not enough to just use the channels you own/control or the ones that don't cost you.

In order to connect with and market to brand new people you will need to use the channels that are owned or controlled by others. This almost always costs money, and so don't shy away from it. Use it!

It is actually amazing that all you need in order to get onto the channels belonging to other people is money! With some money you open the door to accessing more people in your market. Spending money on marketing allows you to reach the people who would buy from you in the future, and this is what gives you money now and down the road. Spending money on marketing is necessary.

One more point on this, don't just spend for the sake of spending and don't just market for the sake of marketing. You need to ensure it is effective and getting results or it is not worth the money or time. To see if it's getting results you have to let something run for a little bit of time - a one-time mailing or ad is not enough. And when you find something in your marketing that is very effective, pour the money into it.

CHAPTER 18: HOW TO IMPROVE AN ECONOMY

ECONOMY: The financial state of an area. The area can be a particular market, or city, or country, or even the whole planet if someone wanted to look at a bigger picture. When people talk about the economy, they are normally referring to the overall financial state of a physical area (such as the United States or San Diego). In this book we will also look at the word economy as it relates to particular markets, or fields of interest. With the internet, vastly distanced collections of people are able to connect independent of their physical locations, and so this addition to the definition has value.

Most writings on this subject offer direction and advice that has already been tested or is already in use.

If these ideas were already in use, yet the economy they were used in is poor or less than desired, then it can be argued that they are either A) unhelpful in improving that economy or B) a contributing factor to the undesirable state of that economy.

Many things being presented as solutions in today's world are things that have already been used and attempted. Many are currently in use! Some of these might be right, some might be wrong, or all might be wrong.

Such things as: less taxes, more taxes, taxes on the wealthy people, taxes on the less wealthy people, free healthcare, expensive healthcare, free money or welfare, no money in return for work, increasing unemployment, decreasing unemployment, raising the minimum wage, requiring employers to pay benefits, not requiring benefits, requiring expensive education and degrees, not requiring expensive degrees, requiring certifications, etc.

These have all been used and many are currently being used in existing economies and markets. Even with all these wonderful(sarcasm) ideas in use there are many less than desirable economies.

An economy can appear to go poor in a short time span, but rarely do you see one improve as fast.

The smaller the economy, as in less people trading and offering goods or services, the faster it can appear to improve or worsen. The larger the economy the more time it takes for most to feel the impact of the things that influence it.

You, on your own, offering and delivering goods and services have an impact within a market and an impact on the economy of that market. The larger your market share the larger the impact you have. The smaller the market is, the easier it is for you to gain a greater influence and have more of an impact.

Your impact can be good, or it can be bad - but the more individual people you affect the more of an impact you create.

So, your first step to improving an economy within a market or area is to have a service or product offering and get it out there. Sell to people, give them the things they demand.

This is a fresh concept!

Most tell you about going out and spending your money locally. Buy local! Go to the local store, instead of online. Don't care if it costs more.

What I am telling you here is not the opposite of that, but it is a new point of view and a different approach.

The condition of an economy is not determined simply by how much money is injected into it, or that could be injected into it. This is far less obvious to notice than the easy and frequently proposed solution of, "just throw more money at it."

"*What?!*" you say. This might seem crazy, I get it. Read on.

As we went over in Chapter 13 on the banker, there's no limit on how much money that can be printed and tossed into a country. Over $3 Trillion was printed and added into the U.S. Economy in 2020. Did this improve the economy? No! At the time of this writing some researchers are reporting over 30% of Americans are unable to afford their rent and are behind on payments.

If someone gets their money from their work-from-home job that is based outside of their city, and then takes that money and buys local, there is money being put into the city in which they live. But does it improve the economy? It does improve the local business that the money was given to. It does help to ensure that this specific local business is still there a little longer to continue to offer products and goods, and it does help to pay for the employees that work there. In theory this is good for that local economy.

In real life though it occurs differently. There is no actual way to control and contain the money within an area. For a small bunch of individuals focusing on their duty to buy local, they do give money to the local business. But, after it is distributed to employees, the owners, and costs to deliver, then where does the money go? Can it actually be contained to this area? The answer is no. The modern-day trading and exchanges require the trading of resources and money with outside markets and other economies.

Unfortunately, as good as buying local sounds, buying local does not have a significant enough impact on the local economy. This applies to cities, states, countries, and it also applies to markets and industries.

The money within the industry of manufacturing laptop computers cannot be contained to that industry completely. It needs to be traded and exchanged with other industries and markets in order to stay alive.

In order to keep buying local, and keep the money within a zone, it would be necessary to forbid the exchange of money with outside areas. The money would have to be forced to stay within a zone. The amount of regulations necessary to enforce something like this would be massive and would border on oppression.

Just putting money into something is not the answer.

A government constantly creates new money and pumps it into their area. They use debt to banks to create this money. They then use this as a reason to raise taxes on the people to be able to afford the debt, or pay for more things, or avoid future debts. In reality they raise taxes and the raised taxes do not then improve the economy, and neither did the increased debt. The need for more debt still shows up in the future and more debt is taken on. In the U.S. this is evident with the ever-increasing national debt which has been steadily growing since it started being counted.

The money that a government issues to its people is not kept within its people. It leaves the area and goes outside that economy to trade with other areas.

In a single year nearly $500 Billion is sent from people within the U.S. to family and friends outside of the country.

In a year, the people of the U.S. send out goods and services (exports) that earn about $2.5 Trillion, but the American people buy goods and services from outside the U.S. (imports) that total $3 Trillion. That is $2.5 Trillion coming in from outside the U.S. and $3 Trillion going out. This results in a $500 Billion loss. This loss is from spending more on purchasing goods from outside the U.S. than the amount of money being earned from outside. This is somewhat similar to an individual who earns $4,000 in a month but spends $5,000. It doesn't work.

The $500 Billion from people sending money out to family as well as the difference between imports and exports add up to a yearly loss of $1 Trillion to the U.S economy. There is probably more being lost with outside exchanges every year, but I didn't count it all up. There are also government funded projects and organizations that use money, but do not exchange something valuable or return money back to the economy - so there is a loss from these as well.

So again... The solution is not more money. And the solution is not forbidding trading with other markets or economies.

The solution is individuals providing work, services, goods, and exchanges within an area and to areas outside. The individual person and the people as a whole creating goods and services and products and trading them with those around them.

The answer is not more regulations, but encouragement. Encouragement is not done by the government, but by the people amongst each other. A government of an area, as history has continually proven, will consistently change its laws and economic policies.

The solution is not "making jobs" within an area. This does give more money to the people within it, but it's similar to just injecting more money, the money will leave.

Instead of trying to create more money, you focus on trading goods and services. This is done by the people and not the government. The attempts by the government in the past have not had a lasting positive effect on this.

If a small town suddenly had lots of people move in from elsewhere, and these people brought with them their work-from-home jobs there might be a surge in that town's economy. Then again, there might not be. The new people can make it possible for the existing providers of goods and services to deliver more, but it is not guaranteed. The new people might have moved there for a lower cost of living and to be able to add more to their savings. They might be sending money back home as is the case with the $500 Billion sent out of the U.S. to family, who knows. They also might buy the things they need from outside the town.

If the people who lived in the small town before the newcomers came are not exchanging and trading goods and services with one another, their economy will not improve. If the people of the small town are not exchanging goods and services with people outside of their town, the economy will not improve. If they have a sense of community with each other, they would be smart to include and make welcome the new people, then the new people will also be interested in this community and exchange with the rest of the town.

If a town had a ton of people move out of it, the people remaining would need to increase their exchange of goods and services with each other and increase their exchange with people outside their town.

This is the same for businesses, as well as markets and industries. It is the same for states and nations.

It's not the spending of money that drives the economy or the government plans to "make more jobs." *It is the creation and exchanging of goods and services inside and outside of an area.*

This is not handled by regulations or the government, but by the individual person - you.

If you want to improve an economy, deliver excellent service and goods to people within that economy. Get great products to the people outside your area. Improve the delivery and the money will follow. Improve the delivery of goods and services and the economy improves.

You improve the economy by getting the people in it to create goods and services and trade those with each other along with people outside of the area for something else valuable. Simply injecting money into an area does not improve the economy of that area.

It starts with you. Use this book and kick ass in your business and your exchange of goods and services. Make lots of money because you provided lots of valuable things to others.

Help the economy even more by getting other people to do the same.

Educate others on the principles in this book. Help others understand economics and finance, and help them to do better in their work and their lives.

Buy copies of this book and give it to your friends and the people you care about and get them to read it too.

Let's improve the economies of our areas.

CHAPTER 19: THE GOAL

A financial goal is how much money or income someone wants to have and what they want to be able to do with it. It really boils down to the things they want to own and the quality of life they want to have now and in the future, and the money or income needed to pay for these things.

Where do people normally get their financial goals from? Normally it comes from the advice of others. It comes from what family members have had, or what they said they should have.

Your goal is *your* goal. What you want is up to you to decide. It can be as much or as little as you like, but I advise having a high number.

Someone stating you need $1 Million saved up to retire is talking about right-now numbers. What about in 30 years, when today's 35-year-old hits retirement age? Will the same experts still be recommending $1 Million for retirement at this later point in time? Probably not. I bet the recommended number will be much higher.

A safe bet would be to get rich. Make some wealth and keep it. I laid out a simple calculation to see what rich could mean for you. To repeat it here: you can add up all the money you would need to fund everything per the chapter on spending and multiply that by 3. If you can get your income up to that number, you will be wealthy according to your own standards. Having that much income and spending the money on the appropriate allocations ensures your financial stability and future.

With that said, what are your goals? What do you want to have down the road? Have you worked these out for yourself? It bears repeating that you should have your own goals set. No financial expert can do that for you.

When you have your goals in mind and are able to work out how much it will cost to attain those goals, there are two ways to go about achieving them:
1. Have enough saved up in a reserve to fund these goals.
2. Have the income levels above what is necessary to fund these goals.

I recommend focusing on option 2, but if you can do both you will be unstoppable.

But again, your goals are your goals, and how you attain them is up to you.

The traditional investment methods sold and advertised appeal to the person who wants to have a lot but work the least. They sound good and I personally would love it if they were true for all, but it's not true for everybody - only some. The traditional path to retirement or lifestyle of choice sounds excellent, but I want you to get the things you want and so advise putting in the work.

Work out what you want and how much money you need to have, or how much you need to be earning, and then go back through the book again with that in mind.

How much money do you need? What is your financial goal or goals?

This chapter was made the last one so you can look at envisioning your goals now with the new understanding gained from the earlier chapters. With your goal or goals in mind re-read everything, or at least the parts you may need.

You should now be looking at the earlier chapters from the point of view of how to achieve your financial goals, and you will gain more tools and useful information than you might have gotten the first time reading everything.

I am keeping the book short for this purpose. I cover the basics of this subject of economics and left out as many unnecessary words as possible to allow you to read this as many times as needed.

I wish you luck in achieving your goals - kick some ass!

FINISHED THE BOOK - NOW WHAT?

Do these things:

1. Go to:
    www.workingeconomics.com/i-finished-reading-the-book
2. Start your 2nd read-through, as per Chapter 19: The Goal.
3. Please leave a review of this book on Amazon.
4. Contact me (Social media: @AuthorJeremyPS, or www.workingeconomics.com/contact) and tell me:
    - What was your favorite thing in this book?
    - How have you used the data in this book? Any successes?
    - What are you most interested in learning about next?

Here are some more things you can do:

A. Go to www.workingeconomics.com for more on this subject.
B. Find me on social media (@AuthorJeremyPS) and say hello.
C. Tell other people about this book.
D. Buy additional copies of this book to give to other people.
E. Leave reviews on book distributors or review websites.
F. Develop and expand your business.
G. Increase your income.
H. Create wealth.
I. Kick some ass.

ABOUT THE AUTHOR

After being 4 months behind on rent - even though it was only $200 per month, Jeremy decided it was time to learn about making money. He quit his low paying job and taught himself website development over the internet, for free, and used these skills to earn the income he needed to live and to live better. Like many other people, with increased income he started buying more crap. The need for more things increased as time went on and this led to a point where he was six figures in debt (not with home or student loans, but other purchases). Jeremy now decided it was time to buckle down and learn not just how to make money, but how to use it and how to keep it. His debt has since been eliminated.

Jeremy has spent most of his life helping other people and providing volunteer services - including disaster relief overseas. He is a regular guy who decided to tackle and breakdown the subject of economics for himself. After gaining an understanding of economics for himself, he saw the need to help other people understand it as well. After handling his own debts and financial obligations he saw how other people he knew were somehow in more debt and experiencing more financial stress - even though many of them had more stable jobs and were earning more income. He made it his goal to break down this subject and help unscramble it for others.

Made in the USA
Las Vegas, NV
04 January 2021